EVERYDAY ENCOUNTERS WITH GOD

WHAT OUR EXPERIENCES TEACH US ABOUT THE DIVINE

D1007815

Before you the whole universe is as a grain from a balance,
or a drop of morning dew come down upon the earth.

—WISDOM 11:22 (NAB)

EVERYDAY ENCOUNTERS WITH GOD

WHAT OUR EXPERIENCES TEACH US ABOUT THE DIVINE

BENEDICT GROESCHEL, CFR, AND BERT GHEZZI

©2008 Benedict Groeschel, CFR, and Bert Ghezzi
All rights reserved.
Published by The Word Among Us Press
9639 Doctor Perry Road
Ijamsville, Maryland 21754
www.wordamongus.org

12 11 10 09 08 1 2 3 4 5

ISBN: 978-1-59325-139-0

Cover Design by John Hamilton Design

No part of this publication may be reproduced, stored in a retrieval system, or transmitted in any form or by any means—electronic, mechanical, photocopy, recording, or any other, except for brief quotations in printed reviews—without the prior permission of the publisher.
Made and printed in the United States of America.

Acknowledgments are on page 152.

Library of Congress Cataloging-in-Publication Data
Groeschel, Benedict J.
  Everyday encounters with God : what our experience teaches about the divine / Benedict Groeschel and Bert Ghezzi.
       p. cm.
  Includes bibliographical references.
  ISBN 978-1-59325-139-0 (alk. paper)
  1. Spiritual life--Christianity. 2. Experience (Religion) I. Ghezzi, Bert. II. Title.
  BV4501.3.G747 2008
  242--dc22

                                2008022126

CONTENTS

PART THREE / EVERYDAY EXPERIENCES

PART FOUR / REAL PRESENCE

EVERYDAY ENCOUNTERS WITH GOD

As we make our way through life, we are often unaware that God is sending us messages each and every minute of the day. All around us, signs and reminders of God are to be seen. God also speaks to us constantly in our thoughts and inner life. Everywhere the voice of God very gently calls us to turn to him.

We may say, "I'm not aware of such a thing." Of course, that's true of almost all of us. Even though we may have been devout believers all our lives, we may not be sensitive enough to the persistent and ever-present call of God. And a reason we are not aware of God's communicating to us is that we may not watch and listen carefully enough. That's why Jesus challenged us by asking, "Do you have eyes, and fail to see? Do you have ears, and fail to hear?" (Mark 8:18). So the purpose of this book is to awaken us to the countless ways God is speaking to us every day.

Long ago Jacopone di Todi (d. 1306), a great medieval Franciscan poet, said that we live as people locked in a castle, and that God tries to break through to us by appealing to our sight, hearing, sound, touch, and even smell. The more we become aware that God's love pursues us in this way, the more we will experience the richness of the mercy he wants to show us. And as we let God touch our spirits through our senses, we will begin to practice that mysterious art called contemplation. Contemplation is nothing more than a constant awareness of the presence of God as we go about our daily lives.

In recent years, there has been a great deal of writing and interest in contemplation. This is all for the best. However, too often people are preoccupied with mastering techniques of contemplative prayer. We need to be occupied with listening to God and not simply listening to ourselves. Paying attention to God's voice is the essence of contemplation. He can speak to us through our desires and our inner experiences as well as through the world around us. God is calling us, and the basic technique of contemplative prayer is to learn how to listen to him.

In this book, we will explore different ways that God is communicating to us. (The author of the chapter will be identified at the end of the selection.) We have written about our world, our humanness, our relationships, our experiences, our spirituality, our life in the Christian community, and much more. A reflection question has been included to provide you with a way to pray and meditate on that specific way that you can encounter the Lord. In addition, each of the five sections ends with additional questions so that you can gather with others to discuss the issues that are raised.

Our hope is that our witness will open you to the numerous and diverse ways God is trying to get your attention. For as St. Paul declared to the Athenians, "In him we live and move and have our being" (Acts 17:28). God gives us all that we have. He joins with us, not only in the beautiful aspects of life, but also in our trials and troubles. His coming to us is called grace. This is a book about how to recognize the call of God's grace in our lives.

—BENEDICT J. GROESCHEL, CFR
—BERT GHEZZI

Part One

ALL AROUND US

CHAPTER ONE

SILENT SPEAKERS

THE NATURAL WORLD TELLS US ABOUT GOD

Ever since the creation of the world his eternal power and divine nature,
invisible though they are, have been understood and seen
through the things he has made.

—ROMANS 1:20

Almost everyone thinks of St. Francis of Assisi as someone who found God in nature. And it is certainly true that St. Francis, particularly in his beautiful Canticle of the Sun, shows a person eminently sensitive to God's call in the material world. Here, for example, he praises the sun, moon, and stars. "O Lord," sings Francis, "omnipotent and good!"

> We honor, praise, and bless you as we should. . . .
> To you be praise through all that you have done—
> Through creatures all, and first through Brother Sun!
> Of you he is a symbol, beauteous, bright;
> He makes the day and gives us warmth and light.
> Praise too through Sister Moon and ev'ry Star
> Which you have made to shine in Heav'n afar.[1]

St. Bonaventure, who succeeded St. Francis as general of the Franciscans, also discerned the divine in nature and wrote a lovely book called *The Footprints of God in Creation.*

However, many of us don't live in close proximity to the natural world in its purist form. We live in towns and cities. We are surrounded by artifacts. Sometimes we sit in a room where there isn't a single thing in its natural state—where everything has been manufactured. Maybe the closest we can get is a cold winter night, sitting in front of a fireplace where the logs, and nothing else, came from nature.

The sterility of our urban environments explains why people seeking to be contemplatives often have chosen to live in rural places. Monasteries and convents are frequently built in the woods or the wilderness. What about the rest of us who have to drive on the freeways or take the bus or the subway? Where can we find God's presence, power, and beauty reflected in nature?

When he was in a Nazi concentration camp, Viktor Frankl, the renowned psychiatrist and author of *Man's Search for Meaning,* said that the only thing that reminded him of God and reality was the sky. The Nazis had not taken away the clouds by day and the stars by night. And so, he turned his thoughts and senses to the sky where he could perceive the beauty of God. Thankfully, most of us are not in such a situation.

The sky, the sea, the sunset, the sunrise, or the earth around us can astonish us with the beauty of God. While you are reading this book, I urge you to find a little piece of the natural world, even if you live in a big city. It may be that you have the prairie outside your window, a pond across the street, a park down the block, or maybe you only have a window box. But stop and look at what God has made.

People become confused and imagine that God made the world much like a contractor builds a house. But God works differently. He creates things in an evolutionary way. Thus, St. Augustine reminds us that God has put into all things the seeds of their growth, development, and ultimate reality. He taught that God made the world like a bud that opens gradually and follows the pattern of life that it had in its most seminal form. Look around you, and you will see not only the beauty of what God has made but the intricacy with which he has made it.

Think about the conception of a baby. At one point, there are only two tiny realities that become one and form the zygote or fertilized egg. Yet all of the future development of that child is there. Not only are the child's gender and physical characteristics contained in the zygote's DNA, but also the child's future affinity for such things as music, fiction, or gardening. These preferences, which appear to be decisions we make on our own, are instead often the products of heredity, and we don't even realize it.

Think of your own mysterious life—how it goes on and how it is preserved. And then you will be inclined to fall on your knees and realize that you have been living in a temple of God all these years and didn't know it.

—FR. BENEDICT

For Reflection:

Think back to a time when a natural setting made you aware of God. How did God speak to you in that setting?

CHAPTER TWO

THE HEAVENS

REVEALING GOD'S GREATNESS

The heavens declare the glory of God;
the sky proclaims its builder's craft.

—PSALM 19:2 (NAB)

One night around twenty-two hundred years ago, somewhere near Alexandria, Egypt, the writer of the Book of Wisdom lay back on his lawn, his head cushioned on his arms, and stared awestruck at the starry heavens. We have probably all done this at one time or another. Like him, we share in his wonderment as we behold the cosmic light show and recognize our littleness in the presence of such a gigantic universe. Also like him, we try to imagine the One who created such an immeasurable and beautiful marvel.

The next morning when our Wisdom author got to his desk, he looked for just the right metaphor to express the greatness of the Creator. He thought that to God the universe might seem like a grain of wheat that falls from a farmer's scale, or like a dewdrop our writer saw that morning on a lotus flower in his pond. So he took up his pen and wrote: "Indeed, before you the whole universe is as a grain from a balance, or a drop of morning dew come down upon the earth" (Wisdom 11:22, NAB). By reducing the vast world to the tiniest images, he magnified the unimaginable power of God.

The writer conceived the universe as the Book of Genesis described it. A dome or "firmament," like an inverted bowl, covered the land and the seas of the earth. The sun, moon, and stars were attached to the firmament as "lights in the dome of the sky" (Genesis 1:14).[2] This universe appeared enormous to him, but he had no idea how big it really is.

We know now that the earth is a planet that orbits around the sun and that our sun is a star—one of billions of stars in a galaxy called the Milky Way. We also know that the Milky Way is one of fifty to one hundred billion galaxies, each of which has its billions of stars. Scientists estimate that, all told, the universe has about one hundred billion trillion stars.[3] Written in figures, that's 100,000,000,000,000,000,000,000—a number so huge that our minds cannot begin to grasp it. I would love to have witnessed the astonishment of the Wisdom author when he got to heaven and someone reported these facts to him.

And there are more realities that would have boggled our author's mind. (They boggle mine.) The galaxies and their stars are spread over an unimaginable expanse of space. The distances among them are so great that for convenience's sake, astronomers measure them in terms of light-years rather than miles. Light travels at 186,282 miles per second or about six trillion miles in a whole year.

According to this standard of measurement, Proxima Centauri, the star nearest our solar system, is 4.2 light-years or more than 25 trillion miles away from the earth.[4] Andromeda, the closest galaxy to the Milky Way, is 2.5 million light years from us. And the most distant galaxies so far discovered by astronomers are an astounding 14 billion light-years from the earth.[5] If you want to express that distance in miles, you do the math. Upon hearing this news, our Wisdom author would have prostrated himself before God's throne. When I think about it, I want to fall on my face and join him.

The author of Wisdom may have had an inkling about the beginnings of the universe. "Not without means," he wrote, "was your almighty hand, that had fashioned the universe from formless matter" (Wisdom 11:17, NAB). Scientists tell us that about 15 billion years ago, the universe began to expand from a pinpoint of compressed potential. It was a speck (of "formless matter"?) billions of times smaller and denser than a single atom, whose energy was equivalent to all the energy and matter of the cosmos today. The speck exploded in a "Big Bang," from which unfolded the immense and ever-expanding universe.

The Big Bang sent the cosmos crashing outward at an inconceivable speed. Yet the timing of the creative outburst was exactingly controlled. If the Big Bang had been slightly less violent and the initial expansion had been even a tad slower, the universe would have collapsed back on itself, the first matter and energy receding back into the primordial speck. If the Big Bang had been slightly more violent and the expansion had been a tad faster, the initial elements would have moved too rapidly to have allowed the formation of stars. We are talking here about tiny fractions of seconds.[6] And as George F. Will once observed, "The odds against us were—this is just the right word—astronomical."[7] But it seems to me that Someone knew exactly what had to be done and exactly what he was doing.

Now we come to the most astounding truth about the origin of the heavens. Science cannot tell us where the speck was before the Big Bang. It was not hanging in the vast void we call space. The universe created space as it expanded. Before the initial explosion, there was no space, no boundless abyss, no darkness, no place for the speck to be. There was no *where*. And so all the great expanse of the starry heavens came to be from *nothing*. I suspect that this thought gave our Wisdom author goose bumps, as it does me. It is this fact more than the enormity of the universe itself—the fact that God created it all from nothing—that proclaims unequivocally his greatness.

—BERT

For Reflection:

What does the creation of the universe tell you about what God is like?

CHAPTER THREE

THREE BIRTHS

REFLECTING GOD'S LOVE

For it was you who formed my inward parts;
you knit me together in my mother's womb.

—PSALM 139:13

Our parish conducts baptisms during Sunday Mass. After the homily, Fr. Charlie, our pastor, who has a superb liturgical sense, baptizes babies with a warm and dramatic flair. At the conclusion of the ceremony, he holds up the infant and introduces little Luke or little Lily—"washed all fresh and clean and fragrant with blessed oil"—as our new brother or sister. The parish welcomes the children with extended applause.

Last Sunday when Father presented a newly baptized child to the parish, it occurred to me that as Christians, we actually celebrate three births: our birth into this world, our birth into the church, and our ultimate birth into heaven. And each of these births is a sign that reflects God's love for us.

Thanks to modern technology and genetic biology, we now know a lot more about conception and natural birth—what I've called the "first birth"—than my wife and I knew when each of our seven children was born. We know, for example, that only one of about three million of the dad's sperm unites with the mom's egg to create the single cell that will develop into a baby. God's precision and profligacy are astounding. A few hours later, the cell begins to divide—not wildly but controlled by special genes—into the complex systems that will become a little human being. Here is an analogy that makes the point:

> Imagine yourself as the world's tallest skyscraper, built in nine months and germinating from a single brick. As that brick divides, it gives rise to every other type of material needed to construct and operate the finished tower—a million tons of steel, concrete, mortar, insulation, tile, wood, granite, solvents, carpet, cable, pipe and glass as well as all furniture, phone systems, heating and cooling units, plumbing, electrical wiring, artwork and computer networks, including software.[8]

Can anyone not be amazed at the progressive development of the fetus?

> —At one month, no bigger than a ladybug, the embryo forms a primitive heart, eyes, blood vessels, and brain.
> —At two months, no bigger than a grape, all the fetus's major organs are in place, ready to grow: brain, heart, stomach, liver, esophagus, kidneys, lungs, and vertebrae.
> —At three months, the fetus has developed a rib cage, eyes, and ears. It can even suck its thumb.[9]

By seven months the fetus's development is almost complete. Just a little more growth, and in two months the baby will be ready to emerge from the world of the womb into our world.

So God allows two infinitesimally small cells to unite and become a girl or boy, woman or man. In effect, he creates us from nothing! In the face of these wonders, awe is the only possible emotion.

Jesus once spoke about the "second birth" with Nicodemus, a Jewish leader who approached him secretly at night (John 3:1-8). Jesus opened the conversation by asserting that "no one can see the kingdom of God without being born from above."

Astonished, Nicodemus asked, "How can anyone be born after having grown old? Can one enter a second time into the mother's womb and be born?"

"I tell you," said Jesus, "no one can enter the kingdom of God without being born of water and the Spirit." This enigmatic response seems to have confused Nicodemus, who left the scene, muttering, "How can these things be?"

Jesus was speaking of the new birth that happens at baptism, when we are received into the church. Our baptism is a death, which is a prelude to new life (see Romans 6:4). We shed our old nature and take up a new one, becoming a new creation (see 2 Corinthians 5:17). I think this second birth roughly parallels the birth of a baby, who leaves behind the comfort of the womb and launches into a new life in a strange but wonderful world. So when I witness infant baptisms at Mass, I marvel at God's love, which makes us new creations that share his very life.

On Christmas morning 2006, my friend Elizabeth, then ninety-eight years old, said to her nurse, "It's time," and then she died. She seemed to have known, or perhaps even to have chosen, the time for her death. Elizabeth did not fear her passing from this life because she understood a fact that many of us tend to forget. She knew that death was not the annihilation of her person—only a temporary separation of her spirit from her body.

Our death is really a "third birth." It is our passage from life on this beautiful earth to an unimaginably better life in heaven. Just as after nine months a baby emerges from the comfortable darkness of a mother's womb into the world, in death we emerge from the womb of this world—poets have called it the Father's womb[10]—into the inconceivably wondrous world of heaven.

When my mother died, I pictured her with a golden crown adorning her silver hair, dressed in a shimmering golden gown, and dancing on a golden street. I hold this image of my mother—who gave me my first birth and then arranged for my second birth—as a sign of God's love for me, a promise of the joy to come when I experience my third birth.

—BERT

For Reflection:

How often do you think of your baptism as a second birth and your death as a third birth? How does thinking of baptism and death in this way change your perception of them?

CHAPTER FOUR

THE HUMAN BODY

CELEBRATING GOD'S GIFT

I praise you, for I am fearfully and wonderfully made.
—PSALM 139:14

As I sit at my computer, sipping coffee, staring at the screen, and then tapping my fingers on the keyboard, a million things are going on. My brain's electrical impulses are telling my fingers where to type as my eyes relay the words on the screen back into my brain. I savor the taste of the coffee. I take deep breaths and pray for ideas and inspiration to change formless thoughts into the written word.

Like most people, I am often oblivious to the wonders of my body. Sure, I find plenty to complain about. When I was a teenager, I hated that I was only five-foot-five and not very good at sports. My small stature and lack of athletic ability gave me a severe case of adolescent low self-esteem. At sixty-six years old, I am well over feeling bad about myself. (Some friends tell me that over the years, I have overcorrected the problem!) But now I have new complaints. Why do I gain weight every time I even look at sweets and fatty foods? And why is it so hard for me to get off my duff and go for a walk?

And yet here I sit, a bundle of a hundred trillion cells, each one encoded with DNA that maps out who I am, a person with a body unlike any other that has ever walked the earth—or ever will. And my body is smart. I don't have to tell my heart to beat or my lungs to breathe. My body sends me signals to eat when I'm hungry and to sleep when I'm tired. It often knows how to heal itself.

Christianity has often been accused of denigrating the human body, but in fact the church holds a very positive view of the body, soul, and spirit that constitute the human person. Pope John Paul II thought so much of the body, in fact, that he wrote a *theology* of the body, which says that the body reveals the mystery of God. "The body, and it alone," he said, "is capable of making visible what is invisible: the spiritual and the divine. It was created to transfer into the visible reality of the world the mystery hidden since time immemorial in God, and thus be a sign of it."[11]

God is pure spirit, but he loved us so much that he sent us the revelation of himself in Jesus. So we can know God through Jesus, who had a body just like ours. He got hungry, tired, and maybe even cranky. He suffered bodily pains. Now God has a face. And the way we can come to know God is through our bodies. That's why we celebrate the sacraments. Sacraments are, after all, concrete and tangible ways to God. The water, the oil, the bread, the wine, the touch, the words—all are experienced through our senses. And yet they bring us face-to-face with the invisible reality of God and his mercy and grace.

God not only designed and created our human bodies, but he also wants us to have them forever. Death was never his plan, and although we will someday say good-bye to our bodies as we know them, our Father promises something even better. Someday we will be like Jesus, resurrected from the dead, with glorified bodies even more wonderful than the ones we have now.

As I age, I am sometimes disappointed at the changes I observe in my body, like when I can't remember somebody's name or the word that is on the tip of my tongue, or when I get short of breath running up a few stairs. Yet I appreciate my body more, not less. My amazement grows when I realize that it has served me well. And it keeps on working, helping me to collaborate with the Lord to advance his kingdom. My body is the temple of my spirit *and* the Holy Spirit, and God can use my body to bring his light to others—through a smile, a hug, a kind word, a meal prepared, or a hand laid on another person in prayer.

So without getting obsessed, I am more and more dedicated to treating my body well. I try to get enough sleep. I try to eat low-fat, healthy foods, and I skip desserts most of the time. Perhaps most important, I try to de-stress by looking for the humor in things and laughing at my foibles. I don't want to mistreat this body, which is God's gift and instrument. I want to be able to use my body as long as possible in his service.

God is a brilliant designer, brilliant beyond all imagination. He gifts us with a body and asks us to use it for his glory. He provides us with nourishment and rest. Most of all, he sent his Son to become one of us, a man with a human body that is wonderful and useful and fragile and capable of suffering and subject to death. And through that death, God tells us not to worry. The power that raised Jesus from the dead will someday raise us from the dead. Then we will have bodies for eternity, perfect bodies that don't age, sin, get fat, or deteriorate. I can't wait!

—BERT

For Reflection:

In what ways do you appreciate your body as God's gift to you, both for yourself and as a way to serve him?

CHAPTER FIVE

A CLOUD OF WITNESSES

TESTIFYING TO GOD'S PRESENCE

Since we are surrounded by so great a cloud of witnesses, . . . let us run with perseverance the race that is set before us.

—HEBREWS 12:1

In Psalm 139, David depicts God as both transcendent and immanent, a God who is both distant from us and simultaneously close to us. God's ways are so far above us, he says, that trying to count his thoughts would be like counting every grain of sand on every seashore. And that would just barely get us started (see Psalm 139:17-18).

Yet God is so present to us, and we to him, that he knows each of our thoughts before we think them (see Psalm 139:2, 4). With David, we can celebrate his nearness and delight in his unexpected touch: "You hem me in, behind and before, and lay your hand upon me" (139:5). The transcendent God who created the universe with a word and the immanent God who walked and conversed with Adam and Eve in the garden (see Genesis 1 and 3) is the same God who gently makes himself known to us—often through other people whom we encounter each day.

We are, in fact, surrounded by witnesses who crowd around us, testifying to the Lord's presence and involvement in our lives. Just in the past month, for example, I can recall a host of such witnesses, who drew my attention to God's presence and engaged me with his initiatives. I bumped into them in books, magazines, on the Internet, at work, in church, and among my friends. Let me tell you about them.

I begin my morning routine by reading about the saint of the day. These heroes of the faith always jump-start my spirit. But two saints I encountered last week made me especially aware of God's action in our lives. Jesuit St. Peter Claver (1580–1654) spent forty years at Cartagena, New Grenada, now Colombia, caring for hundreds of thousands of slaves imported from West Africa. Day and night he fed, bathed, and brought medical aid to slaves chained in wretched hovels. He acted as God's angel of mercy, bringing them bread, lemons, medicines, brandy, tobacco, and cologne—and the gospel. I also met St. Catherine of Genoa (1447–1510), another sign of God's mercy in two senses: compassion and care. Catherine forgave her unfaithful husband and his mistress. Then, with her repentant husband, she cared for the sick at one of Europe's largest hospitals for a quarter of a century.[12]

Last week my friend Henry Libersat set up another divine encounter for me. He gave me a copy of *Miracles Do Happen*, which he coauthored with Sr. Briege McKenna, OSC. The book tells the story of Sr. Briege's miraculous healing, which was the beginning of her extraordinary healing and evangelistic ministry. As a young nun, she suffered from an aggressive case of rheumatoid arthritis, which crippled her and destined her to life in a wheelchair. But at a retreat in 1967 where she was simply seeking spiritual renewal, God instantly healed her of the disease. Then he called her to a ministry of healing and spiritual renewal for priests. For four decades, she has conducted healing services and led prayer meetings throughout the world.[13]

Other witnesses reported evidence of God's compassion on the sick. I learned that two of my friends were healed of cancer through a combination of prayer and medical interventions.

Eight months ago, my longtime friend Dick contracted an aggressive form of prostate cancer. We barraged heaven for his healing, and he received the Sacrament of Anointing of the Sick. A gifted doctor was able to extract the infected gland, leaving no trace of cancer and causing only minimal side effects. This month Dick resumed his regimen of running several miles daily and his full load of college teaching.

Joan spoke at a parish eucharistic healing service. She told how twenty-five years ago, shortly after her marriage, she experienced back pain so severe that she could only lie flat on her back. Doctors discovered a tumor woven about her vertebrae and predicted that she would never bear children. Family and friends bathed Joan in prayer and gathered around her at Mass to pray for her healing. When doctors opened up her back, the tumor "popped" out of her spine, so they were able to remove it entirely. Joan recovered completely and now has seven children.

Yesterday a brochure from Cross International introduced me to two nuns who bear daily witness to God's loving presence. Cross International is a Florida-based Catholic agency that supports missions throughout the world. I learned about Sr. Estella and Sr. Myrna, both Missionary Sisters of the Poor in the Philippines. Sr. Estella is a nurse who devotes herself to caring for severely handicapped children. Sr. Myrna serves the poor who are very near death. What struck me most was her story of how a dying man had blessed her:

> One of the men who was very close to death was sitting up in bed, and his whole body was shaking. I prayed to God for guidance. What came to mind was a blanket—the Lord was calling me to wrap the man and embrace him. As I wrapped him with the blanket and held him, he shook and swayed.

I could also hear him murmuring, but I couldn't tell what he was saying. . . . I finally realized that he was praying. He said, "Lord, bless this lady. Bless the sister. Bless her, Lord." I was so humbled in that moment. The man's selfless love was amazing. Even at the point of death he was praying for others than himself.[14]

Finally, two books I came across this month helped me see something about God. I was deeply moved by the seventh volume in the Harry Potter series. In that book, Harry freely lays down his life in order to do battle with a diabolical enemy who is trying to take over the world.[15] When I put the book down, I felt I had learned that God wants me always to freely choose to do the right thing, no matter the cost. I was touched even more by the witness of Mother Teresa's personal writings in *Come Be My Light*.[16] Her faithful service for decades without any sense of God's presence taught me that the Lord cherishes obedience in his disciples more than anything else.

Now my challenge is to put these lessons into practice. And I invite you to look beyond the ordinary, where you will find traces of God's presence in the witness of those you encounter each day.

—BERT

For Reflection:

In the recent past, what witnesses have made God present to you?

CHAPTER SIX

THE MAJESTY OF ART AND ARCHITECTURE

PROCLAIMING GOD'S BEAUTY

*The acute experience of great beauty readily evokes a nameless yearning
for something more than earth can offer. Elegant splendor reawakens
our spirit's aching need for the infinite, a hunger for more
than matter can provide.*

—THOMAS DUBAY[17]

Art and architecture represent visually the highest accomplishments
of human creativity. Behind both of these and any other artistic presentation, such as music, is the genius that God has given to certain
people. All of their creations reflect their relationship to the divine
artist. They are all meant to be works of God.

As a youngster of six years old, my grandmother, an intrepid
tourist, took my siblings, cousins, and me to the Metropolitan
Museum of Art and the Museum of Natural History. From the
rather grimy, industrial city where we lived, she brought us to
Manhattan and showed us very ancient and beautiful paintings.
My grandmother's favorite museum was the Frick Gallery, where
Bellini's marvelous painting *St. Francis in Ecstasy* hangs on the wall
next to Holbein's splendid portrait of St. Thomas More.

At first I used to think, "Just another art museum." But gradually I came to realize that I was being favored with visits to
most unusual places. For right across the river, we had access

to some of the greatest museums in the world. My favorite was the Cloisters, a medieval monastery dismantled and reassembled in a park in northern Manhattan. When you enter this lovely museum, you might think that you have traveled back in time to the thirteenth century. It is crammed with the art of the medieval Catholic Church, especially the art of Catholic devotion. Along with the medieval galleries of the Metropolitan Museum of Art, the Cloisters truly shows you the art and genius of the medieval Catholic Church.

When I went as a teenager to visit the museums, I felt like I was going to church. The art museums and their magnificence seemed to be visual catechisms proclaiming the dogmas of the Catholic faith. Almost every great artist up to the seventeenth century depicted scenes of the life of Christ or presentations of the mysteries of faith. Even after that time, the great artists of the world often portrayed reality in such beautiful ways that the glory of God can be seen. For example, the Hudson River School, a group of mainly Protestant artists, painted natural scenes along the Hudson Valley with trans-figuring light shining through them. Art critics have said that all of these works, which show the river and the boats, the trees and the flowers, are really works of religious art.

If you ever get the chance to visit these marvelous museums, make sure you take the opportunity to do so. If you can, spend more than one day there. Take your time, and try to separate yourself from the crowd, so that you can pause and contemplate the wondrous works that human beings have created to repre-sent the beauty of God.

Art is supposed to be a mirror of life. Unfortunately, some artists do not mirror life, or if they do, the mirrors they use are broken. Some of this artwork even reminds me of graffiti, and it is ultimately a pretense. When art or architecture or music is used to corrupt people or to draw them away from God, it is a rather hideous distortion of what God has made when he created the human mind and its abilities.

Much the same can be said of architecture. Buildings that are going to be used for evil purposes are often conceived in hideous and ugly ways, like the barracks at concentration camps or the slave cities of Siberia. But as soon as the evil is over, people will try to build beautiful structures in these places. I think of the lovely Convent of the Holy Blood, which has as its spire the gun tower of the Dachau concentration camp. The interior of the convent very much follows the lines of a barracks. Yet it is there that the nuns pray for the souls who perished at the hands of the Nazis and even for the salvation of those who tortured and slaughtered so many people.

Art and architecture can preach. We ought to see what they are preaching. We should be sensitive to their message. When we look at a painting or a building, we should ask, "What is its creator trying to say to me?" Some modern art and architecture are cynical, and their purpose is ultimately nihilistic, declaring that there is no meaning and no beauty. Perhaps in our lifetime, we are going to see an end to that notion and its reflection in art. Because of Jesus, life does have meaning and beauty. Magnificent art and architecture proclaim that meaning and beauty in a way that speaks to our hearts.

—FR. BENEDICT

For Reflection:

What one work of art or architecture has most affected you? In what way did it make you think of God?

QUESTIONS FOR GROUP DISCUSSION

1. What are some things about God that you learn from observing the natural world? How do these insights affect you?

2. How does knowledge about the science of the universe increase your faith?

3. In what ways do you think our birth into heaven at death compares to our birth into this world?

4. What does reflecting on the wonders of the human body tell you about God?

5. What person, place, or thing has taught you something about God?

6. How can we grasp what God may be saying to us through a beautiful painting or building?

Part Two

A LOOK IN THE MIRROR

CHAPTER SEVEN

LONGINGS

THIRSTING FOR GOD

Lord, you called to me and cried aloud, and you broke through my deafness. You flashed, and shone, and chased away my blindness. You breathed upon me fragrantly; I drew in my breath, and now I pant for you. I tasted, and now I hunger and thirst for you. You touched me, and I burned to enjoy your peace.

—AUGUSTINE[1]

When I was in school, Sr. Dolorita told us that the *Confessions of St. Augustine* was one of the great books of Catholic history. I quickly took myself to the local public library and borrowed the only available copy. It was a nineteenth-century Anglican translation, written in beautiful but rather stilted language. And I immediately started to read it.

The first paragraph practically knocked me on the ground. Even in the angular prose of the translation, these words struck me: "Thou hast made us for Thyself, O God, and our hearts are restless until they rest in Thee." I can easily say that much of my life has been organized around this sentence, along with several lines from the Sermon on the Mount. "Our hearts are restless"—how true this seemed, even to a fourteen-year-old boy. And I would say, now sixty years later, that it seems even more true than it did then.

Human beings are in a perpetual search for happiness. This is the way that God has made us. Unfortunately and mysteriously, the discord of life that comes from original sin leads us to long for and look for our fulfillment in lesser realities. Indeed, our hearts will not find rest until they rest in God.

We desire God, not only because the thought of possessing him is so tremendously beautiful and fulfilling, but also because we realize that our stay in this world is temporary. We are well aware that we are headed beyond this world to eternal life. The words of the Old Testament, "You shall seek the LORD, your God; and you shall indeed find him when you search after him with your whole heart and your whole soul" (Deuteronomy 4:29, NAB), are absolutely as meaningful to us today as they were to Israel when they were written thousands of years ago.

In the spiritual life, we need to focus our longings on God. Many times we must look for him through intervening things, such as love of other human beings, passion for the work we do, and enjoyment of the legitimate pleasures of life. It's wrong to think that if you desire God, you cannot enjoy anything else. This has often been a mistake in Christian asceticism. In fact, the true lover of God finds him and loves him even in things that he has made. Think of the longing behind a good marriage, in which husband and wife find their road to God through the love of each other and the love of their children. This is why marriage is a sacrament, a sign of grace. Think of the love that a person may experience for the sick, for the poor, or for the marginalized. Consider the love that people may have for their country or for a good cause to which they have dedicated themselves.

Danger comes only when our longings are simply for material things, which do not last and can pass away in the blink of an eye. In biblical language, this is called vanity, meaning love that goes toward nothing.

If we examine our lives from the viewpoint of the gospel, especially by the words of our Lord in the Sermon on the Mount and in the parables, we will see a very clear direction for orienting our desires. We will discover that we may reach our goal of possessing God in unexpected ways—by seeking to set things right in the world, by enduring persecution, by loving our enemies, and by repairing broken relationships. By following the teachings of the gospel, we will come to know indeed that God has made us for himself. And, we will also know that our hearts are restless until they rest in him.

—FR. BENEDICT

For Reflection:

Which of your good desires, if you pursue them, will lead you more fully to God?

Chapter Eight

Mothers and Fathers

Images of God

A child is not likely to find a father in God unless he finds something of God in his father.

—Austin L. Sorenson

The woman who creates and sustains a home, and under whose hands children grow up to be strong and pure men and women, is a creator second only to God.

—Helen Hunt Jackson

I learned some things about our Father in heaven from my father and mother on earth. That's the way it is for many of us. We tend to project onto God the behaviors and attitudes of our parents. Some criticize this tendency as being anthropomorphic. But call it what you like, we do shape God in our parents' image, and we often do it unconsciously.

And yet, there are many qualities exhibited by loving parents that we can also attribute to God. When mothers and fathers take delight in their children, we can easily imagine our Father taking delight in us. Parents who care for, protect, nourish, and love their children—even when they misbehave—reflect qualities of a God who does all this for his children and more. In fact, our most basic relationship to God is one of parent to child. We call God "Father," not only because that is what Jesus called him, but also because that is the most appropriate metaphor in our limited human language that we can find for him.

My father died of a heart attack when I was twelve years old, but I am blessed with memories of him that have helped me to know God's love. Dad enjoyed many good things in life—making things with his hands, hearty meals, sports, a cold beer—but nothing delighted him more than our family. Every morning as he was leaving for work, he gathered us and roughed us up with boundless affection.

Dad was also a great provider. The eldest son of a poor Italian coal miner, he had endured poverty and the deprivations of the Great Depression and World War II. Like many in his generation, he was determined to ensure that his family would not suffer as he had. So he worked long days as a carpenter and for several years worked evenings and weekends building our home.

One time my father rescued me and my sister from certain death. Dad's saving us is my clearest memory of him. We were waiting for him in his pickup truck when the emergency brake gave way. The truck lurched into gear and was about to roll down a steep hill into a gully. Exerting what seemed like superhuman effort, Dad managed to chase and mount the truck and stop it. I also remember that I was so sure that he would save us that I was not at all afraid.

God loves without limit. I first grasped the meaning of limitless love by watching how my mother loved. Like Dad, Mom was also a child of a poor, large immigrant Italian family. The next to youngest of seven children, she learned how to make do with little and share what she had. After our dad's early death, she raised me, my two sisters, and my brother as a single parent in a remarkably unselfish way. Mom gave her all to provide us with a comfortable life. She deprived herself of ordinary needs and pleasures to feed and clothe us, maintain our home, and send us to parochial schools. I lived at home for eleven years after my dad died, and I cannot remember her ever eating out at a restaurant or going to a movie.

Then there was the food. Mom delighted in nourishing our bodies—and in doing so, she nourished our spirits as well. No one could escape our house without eating. There was always pasta, pizza, fried chicken, chocolate cake with chocolate frosting and walnuts, pineapple-filled bars, and butterscotch brownies. She presided over her bountiful table with cheerful warmth. My longtime friends still remember her lilting laughter, the sign of her joyful care and affection. Her desire to feed me in this way makes me realize how much the Lord desires to feed me in prayer and at Mass in Scripture and the Eucharist.

Wisdom, guidance, accessibility, protection, and friendship: these are attributes of God that we often seek in mothers, fathers, and spiritual mentors. In my late teens, feeling the loss of my own father, I was on a "father hunt." And I found a spiritual father at college in a professor who reached out to me. Although busy as a teacher and head of his department, he always had time for me. Often at the end of a school day, I would drop in his office for a chat. In those hours, he became my first adult friend, although at the time I regarded him more as a mentor. We talked about everything—the church, family, liturgy, saints, war and peace, sex, politics, the poor—you name it. And we talked about me. He was a great listener. I confided in him, and he always advised me wisely.

He introduced me to praying the psalms and to reading Scripture, which have become a framework for my daily life. Occasionally he stabbed me with a probing question that changed my life. Once, for example, he asked me if I experienced God when I prayed. My immediate answer was no. But that night as I prayed, I sensed the Lord drawing so close to me that he seemed to embrace me. Thus my mentor and friend nudged me into a relationship with God that has oriented my life.

Mothers and fathers are such powerful images of God that when children are not blessed with loving parents, they often find it difficult to relate to God. They cannot disentangle him from their experience of their parents. But we can also find the motherly and fatherly qualities that we so crave in adults who, although they are not our biological parents, can become our spiritual parents.

Of course, we know that every mother and father, no matter how loving, in some way distorts the perfect image of God's maternal and paternal qualities. Yet in every parent's love, we catch a glimpse of God and come to understand in a deeper way his love for us.

—BERT

For Reflection:

What do you think your children or others are learning about God from your words and example?

CHAPTER NINE

FRIENDS AND LOVERS

ECHOES OF GOD'S LOVE

Our Gift-loves are really God-like . . . Their joy, their energy, their patience, their readiness to forgive, their desire for the good of the beloved—all this is a real and all but adorable image of the Divine life.

—C. S. LEWIS[2]

It is no small consolation in this life to have someone you can unite with you in an intimate affection and the embrace of a holy love. . . . A person who, though absent in body, is yet present in spirit, where heart to heart you so join yourself and cleave to him that soul mingles with soul and two become one.

—ST. AELRED OF RIEVAULX[3]

C. S. Lewis says that there are two kinds of love characteristic of human beings. Our "need-loves," for such things as companionship or affection, are least like God because God has no needs. But friendship and married love, our "gift-loves," are the most like God. They mirror the Father giving himself to Jesus, Jesus giving himself to his Father, the Father giving his Son to us, and the giving of the Holy Spirit, who flows from both Father and Son, to us.

I detect this image of the divine reality in my relationships with my friends and my wife, and I suspect that there are relationships in your life where you detect the same image. I met both Richard, my close friend, and Mary Lou, my wife, fifty-three years ago at

St. Justin High School in Pittsburgh, Pennsylvania. Richard and I bonded as high-school debate partners. Over these many years, we have stood together, sharing interests in the Catholic faith, liturgy, higher education, raising children, and good reading and writing. Mary Lou and I—then high school sweethearts, now married for forty-four years—see the benefits of our mutual love and care in the lives of our fourteen grandchildren. And of course, all the kids are above average, like the kids at Garrison Keeler's Lake Wobegon.

Richard and I have celebrated good times and have also supported each other through difficult seasons. We have given each other encouragement and advice during painful years when children drifted into rebellion and trouble. We have opened our lives, commiserated over our problems, confessed our weaknesses, and prayed daily for each other. Most recently I had the privilege of championing both Richard and Patricia, his charming wife, through serious but ultimately successful battles with cancer. We have come to share the kind of bond that St. Aelred described in his classic book on spiritual friendship.

Although contemporary culture has cheapened erotic love by equating it with lust, genuine eros—the gift-love of lovers—carries traces of the divine. Scripture sees eros in God's love relationship with us. For example, it presents Jesus as the bridegroom and us, the church, as his bride (see Mark 2:18-20; Matthew 25:1-13). So Jesus, who loved us and gave himself for us (see Galatians 2:20), models the gifting of eros for us.

At our wedding Mass in 1964, Fr. John Hugo, the celebrant, read to Mary Lou and me a serious mandate for our married life that echoed the Lord's sacrificial love for us:

It is most fitting that you rest the security of your wedded life upon the great principle of self-sacrifice. And so you begin your married life with the voluntary and complete surrender of your individual lives in the interest of the deeper and wider life which you are to have in common. Henceforth you belong entirely to each other. You will be one in mind, one in heart, and one in affections. And whatever sacrifices you may hereafter be required to make for the preservation of this mutual life, always make them generously. Sacrifice is usually difficult and irksome. Only love can make it easy; and perfect love can make it a joy. We are willing to give in proportion as we love. And when love is perfect, the sacrifice is complete. God so loved the world that he gave his only-begotten Son (see John 3:16); and the Son so loved us that he gave himself for our salvation.[4]

Mary Lou and I have not always had these words foremost in mind, but I think a review of our married life will show that we have lived sacrificially for each other. We could argue about who has paid the bigger price to make our marriage work, but I say Mary Lou wins hands down. She gave up the comfort of familiar circumstances and friends to follow me for job changes from South Bend, Indiana, to two cities in Michigan, and finally to Winter Park, Florida. Moreover, she left her professional career for the career of family building, staying home with our seven children for twenty-seven years. We have both put up with each other's quirks, faults, and sins, quickly asking for and giving forgiveness. For my part, I gave up leisure and rest to work extra-long days to cover the costs of our big family. Now, in the sunset of our lives, I handle many household matters to free up Mary Lou to enjoy her work as a librarian. Our companionship and lovemaking gently eased the sacrificing, and God's grace made it possible. And we both think that we have imitated God's delight in caring for us in the delight we take in our mutual service.

So our friendships and marriages tell us something about God. He places a high priority on loving relationships both within the Godhead and among his creatures. And to make love work, he shows us how to give of ourselves generously and joyfully to one another.

—BERT

For Reflection:

Reflect on one special friendship. What has it taught you about God?

CHAPTER TEN

WORKERS AND ARTISTS

CO-CREATORS WITH GOD

*The opening page of the Bible presents God as a kind of exemplar
of everyone who produces a work: the human craftsman mirrors the
image of God as Creator. . . . Through his "artistic creativity" man
appears more than ever "in the image of God," and he accomplishes
this task above all in shaping the wondrous "material" of his own
humanity and then exercising creative dominion over the universe
which surrounds him. With loving regard, the divine Artist passes on
to the human artist a spark of his own surpassing wisdom,
calling him to share in his creative power.*

—POPE JOHN PAUL II[5]

"I did it!" exclaimed Nicholas, my two-year-old grandson. For
the umpteenth time, he had built a tower of blocks—which then,
of course, he knocked over and began to rebuild.

Sprawled nearby, Garrett, his three-year-old brother, had created a bright red Elmo in his Disney coloring book. Amazing to
me, he had manipulated his crayon so as not to cross a single line.
"Look what I did, Grandpa," he said.

"Great job, Garrett," I said. "You are one fine little artist."

Even very young children find something eminently satisfying
in being creative. Built into our human natures, planted by God,
and reflecting God is the desire to create, to make something
that will last beyond ourselves. It's not surprising that children

display pride in their work and art. Making things and appreciating them characterize their young human natures.

Unfortunately, as we leave childhood and bury ourselves in the business of living, we can lose the wonder of our own creativity. "All children are artists," said Picasso. "The problem is how to remain an artist" once we grow up.[6] Pressed with the many duties in our lives, we either forget to exercise our creativity or miss opportunities to see our work as a creative endeavor.

We can see this divinely inspired impulse to creativity in great artists. We also observe it in the satisfaction ordinary people take in their work. And if we are paying attention, we notice it in ourselves.

When we think of creative people, we naturally think of great artists. Picasso, for example, was probably the most productive artist of all time. He began at age nine to produce a painting every morning. For the next three quarters of a century, he created in rapid fire more than thirty thousand pieces in a wide variety of media—paper, canvas, metal, stone, and ceramics.[7] We might ask ourselves how we could ever be so creative or prolific. Picasso enjoyed his work, and he might not have worked so hard if he hadn't in some way felt as if in the very act of creating, he was somehow extending the power of God into the world. "Art," he said, "washes away from the soul the dust of everyday life." His advice to others: "Look for a situation in which your work will give you as much happiness as your spare time."[8]

Even if we don't have the natural gifts to become great artists, we can tap into the innate creativity in our beings and express it in our work—however ordinary. In his classic book *Working*, oral historian Studs Terkel interviewed a mason who loved constructing buildings in stone and felt honored to work with his hands. "I take a lot of pride in it," Carl Murray Bates said, "and I do get, oh, I'd say a lot of praise or whatever you want to call it."[9] Bates claimed to remember every house he had built. "All my work," he said, "is set right out there in the open, and I can look at it as I go by. It's something I can see the rest of my life. . . . It's always there. Immortality as far as we're concerned. Nothin' in this world lasts forever, but did you know that stone . . . deteriorates one sixteenth of an inch every hundred years? . . . So that's gettin' awful close."[10] Then he laughed in appreciation of his creativity.

Even in our routine jobs, we can exercise and enjoy our creativity. The church historian and author Paul Johnson has described the creative sense of a laborer who worked in his neighborhood. He wrote, "I sometimes talk to a jovial sweeper, who does my street . . . I asked him if he felt himself creative and he said: 'Oh, yes. Each day they give me a dirty street, and I make it into a clean one, thanks be to God.'"[11]

We can become like that street sweeper and recognize that even in the most mundane jobs, our creativity can bring beauty and order where there was once ugliness and chaos. At home, when we clean the garage, trim and mulch the bushes, redecorate a room, wash and wax the car, or serve a meal that delights the family, we are co-creators with God, making the world sparkle through our efforts. At work or school, don't our spirits soar when we have made a successful presentation, exceeded our goals, written a well-developed report, or been recognized by our superior for outstanding achievement?

Our satisfaction with our creativity springs from a divine element in our nature. Like Nicholas and Garrett, Picasso, Carl Murray Bates, and the street sweeper, we feel a natural pride in our work. We feel like artists. We look at what we have done and say, "Now that's good!" As John Paul II said, we take pleasure in exercising creative dominion over our universe. And we see in our creativity reflections of the Creator of the universe, who viewed all that he had made and saw that it was "very good" (Genesis 1:31).

—BERT

For Reflection:

What one step could you take to become more aware of your sharing in God's creativity?

Chapter Eleven

Setting Things Right

A Divine Hunger

Your law, my God, is deep in my heart.
—Psalm 40:8 (NJB)

You don't have to teach children about fairness and unfairness.
A sense of justice comes with the kit of being human.
We know about it, as we say, in our bones.
—N. T. Wright [12]

When we encounter something wrong, we want to see it set right. That's part of our human nature. Deep within we hunger for justice. We long to see good overcome the evils of our world—the big global evils, such as poverty, discrimination, crime, terrorism, and genocide, as well as personal injustices, which are big to us, such as being cheated, slandered, injured, or abused.

We share with God this desire to set things right. He loves everything he created and wants to repair the damage evil has done to all of his creatures. He installed in our natures a hunger to work with him to overtake evil with good. "I will put my spirit within you," he said, "and make you follow my statutes and be careful to observe my ordinances" (Ezekiel 36:27). Spiritual inertia may prevent us from doing something about evils that we encounter. But we must learn not to resist our natural impulse to see justice done.

We can observe this inborn desire to set things right even in young children. They often demand justice more readily than adults. For example, if you eavesdrop on children at play, you will inevitably hear a boy or girl who has been offended cry, "That's not fair!"

And sometimes a child's unaffected sense of fairness compels adults, who may be inclined to ignore the divine impulse for justice, to act on it. In his moving novel *The Real American,* my friend Richard Easton tells how two eleven-year-old boys caused adults to overcome prejudice, injustice, and violence. In the story, Italian immigrants have moved into a nineteenth-century country town to work in newly opened coal mines. Alarmed by the incursion of foreigners and afraid of imminent change, the local farmers treat the newcomers unjustly. They isolate the miners, mock their language and customs, overcharge them for necessities, threaten them with violence, and otherwise harass them. As the story unfolds, Nathan, a farm boy, and Arturo, who works in the mines, become good friends. The boys eventually bring their families together, both to help some men who have been injured in a mine accident and also to turn away armed thugs who arrive on the scene to prevent a strike. The story ends with the promise that because of the boys' example, justice will prevail in the town, even though the road ahead will be difficult.

I have found additional evidence for our innate hunger for justice in some unexpected places. I relax by reading mysteries, and my favorite detectives—none of them Christian or even believers—are driven to set things right. For example, Rex Stout's Nero Wolfe solves crimes from his Manhattan brownstone, which he runs as a sanctuary of uprightness and a refuge from the world's evils. And Wolfe's sidekick, Archie Goodwin, is a secular saint who always does the right thing to stymie the bad guys. Stout seems to have deliberately named him "A Good One." I admire these two characters so much that my wife more than once has reminded me that they are fictitious and that I should not expect to meet them in heaven. Oh, well.

I have also observed our natural human passion for justice in contemplative saints whom we might have expected to withdraw from the world's wickedness. In fact, the nearer mystics draw to God, the more they seem to work with him to bring good out of evil.

For example, St. Elizabeth of Hungary (1207–1231), a duchess and a mystic, had her husband construct a hospital near their castle in Thuringia. Twice daily she personally went there to minister to the sick. She arranged for food to be distributed every day to the poor of the duchy, and she gave those she served an opportunity to work in exchange for aid. St. Catherine of Genoa (1447–1510), a gifted visionary, tended the sick at a large hospital from 1473 to 1496, and for eleven of those years served as its administrator. Dominican brother St. Martin de Porres (1579–1639), a contemplative from his youth, turned his monastery at Lima, Peru, into a rough prototype of a modern social services center. Hundreds of the city's poor came daily to him for healing, medicines, food, and money. St. Pio of Pietrelcina (commonly known as Padre Pio, 1887–1968) was a stigmatist and miracle worker who opened a world-class hospital for poor people at his monastery at San Giovanni Rotando in the mountains of Southern Italy. I could list many others, but you get the picture—contemplation leads to action.

So we can learn something about God in the hunger for justice that we observe in ourselves, in children, in fiction, and in contemplative saints. God loved his creatures so much that he decided to do something about the evil that had overtaken us and the world. He sent his only Son to reclaim and renew all of his creation. That's what Jesus Christ was doing when he announced that "the kingdom of God is at hand" (Mark 1:15, NAB; see Matthew 4:23-25) He was declaring that in his person, God was overthrowing the forces of evil and setting things right in the world. God was acting through him to release all who were imprisoned in the kingdom of darkness. In short, God was in Christ, rescuing his creation and restoring it.

Jesus invited men and women, including you and me, to collaborate with him in building the kingdom of God. He offered to make us a light to the world, advancing with him God's great reclamation project (see Matthew 4:18-22; 5:14-16) Thus Jesus aimed to exploit the hunger for justice that God had implanted in our hearts.

So the questions we face are these: How are we responding to God's initiative? Do we ignore our hunger for justice? Or do we take action to satisfy it? We must not fool ourselves into thinking that one person can't make a difference in fixing the world's problems. Individuals like William Wilberforce, Martin Luther King, and Desmond Tutu have changed the world for good. We certainly can change our personal worlds by setting things right, one at a time. And, joining together with other Christians in the body of Christ, we can bring God's justice to earth.

—BERT

For Reflection:

What unjust situation might God be putting on your heart? What one thing could you do to help rectify that situation?

CHAPTER TWELVE

REFLECTIONS OF THE DIVINE

MADE IN THE IMAGE AND LIKENESS OF GOD

God said, "Let us make man in our image, in our likeness."
—GENESIS 1:26 (NIV)

We too easily use the word "God" without giving it much thought or adequate reverence. People will say, "Oh, do it, for God's sake" or "Whatever God wants." Or they even use the name of God irreverently. We need to stop and think of whom we are speaking when we say that simple three-letter word. We must speak of God with the same awe that Paul expressed when he extolled God's greatness: "O the depth of the riches and wisdom and knowledge of God! How unsearchable are his judgments and how inscrutable his ways! 'For who has known the mind of the Lord? / Or who has been his counselor?'" (Romans 11:33-34).

Already in the pages of this book we have pondered the mystery of God's immensity. Now we ask ourselves, "What does this reality, the reality of God, tell us about ourselves?" In many ways, we are profoundly different from God. We have a beginning in time. Our human lives will end in time. However, because of God's extraordinary gift—one that by our human nature we do not have—we expect to live a divine life.

Christ has promised us this eternal life, particularly in the Gospel of John. In the fourteenth chapter of that gospel, Jesus said, "In my Father's house there are many dwelling places. If it were not so, would I have told you that I go to prepare a place for you? And if I go and prepare a place for you, I will come again and will take you to myself, so that where I am, there you may be also" (14:2-3). It is only because there is something in human nature that has a spark of divinity that we could possibly hope to have such an eternal destiny. Human beings by their nature pass away, just like all the other creatures of the earth. It is the gift of God, which we know especially and clearly through Christ, that we are called to live forever with him.

Questions about life after death have always intrigued us. Other world religions, particularly those that began far away from Christianity in the Orient, have dealt with these questions. In our society, even those people who are professedly irreligious during times of sickness and death often turn to God. They do so sincerely, facing perhaps for the first time in their lives the contingency and impermanence of human existence.

Since you are reading this book, you are already convinced that we are made in the image and likeness of God. This mysterious, divine spark that is within us is called grace because it is freely given. We ought to think of the life of grace and try to cultivate it by living virtuously. We should acknowledge grace in good people we meet and by example, at least, try to bring those whose lives are far from God to a state of grace.

You don't hear much about grace in the world today. But it is by grace that we are made in the image and likeness of God. Many of us may not realize it, but the church teaches that grace is neither a creature or a thing. It is beyond any *thing* created. Grace is our living relationship with the absolute, infinite, all-holy divine being. And it is in that grace-filled relationship with God that we become even more like him as we repent and conform our lives to the gospel. As Paul says, "You have stripped off the old self with its practices and have clothed your-selves with the new self, which is being renewed in knowledge according to the image of its creator" (Colossians 3:9-10).

—FR. BENEDICT

For Reflection:

In what ways do you see the divine spark of grace at work in your life?

QUESTIONS FOR GROUP DISCUSSION

1. What do you think about the observation that behind your deepest longings is a hunger for God?

2. How has the example of others influenced your important life choices?

3. What do your relationships with friends have in common with your relationship to God?

4. In which of your commitments, pursuits, or activities do you sense that you are a cocreator with God? Why?

5. Think of an injustice that you suffered personally? How did you try to rectify it?

6. What does it mean to you that you are made in the image of God?

Part Three

EVERYDAY EXPERIENCES

CHAPTER THIRTEEN

THE PRESENT MOMENT

DISCOVERING THE POWER OF "NOW"

Our only satisfaction must be to live in the present moment
as if there were nothing to expect beyond it.
—JEAN-PIERRE DE CAUSSADE[1]

That strange little word "now" is the most succinct and common expression of the present moment. Now is a very mysterious idea. Don't ever underestimate it. It moves through time, through the billions of years of the material world, and it moves on toward the end of the world. It comes from the day without yesterday and moves on to the day without tomorrow.

And now is incredibly real. The past is only a memory. Its significance comes from the fact that it has lasting effects into the now. The future is only a conjecture. It may be quite different than what we anticipated. But now is inescapable. It's irreducible. It's there. It's reality. And it is now, in the present moment, that we work out our salvation. Only what we do now has significance for eternity. Not what we have been, because that can be repented. And not what we will be, because that we don't even know and are not responsible for, except in so far as we now make preparations for the future. We steer the rudder of our lives into the future—now.

Throughout Christian history, many spiritual writers have reflected on the importance of now. Teachers who wrote about practicing God's presence have encouraged us to realize that now is the moment when we are present to God. For example, Jean-Pierre de Caussade and Blessed Julian of Norwich in their teaching about acceptance of the divine will emphasized the sacrament of the present moment, in which God's grace is revealed to us by what is happening now.

A person who has been a great sinner can turn to God in the now and completely reverse the direction of his life. A person hoping to do good may suddenly take a detour off the road of virtue and now find himself away from God or even going against God. So now is both the door to the freedom of grace and also to the slavery of sin.

Perhaps the sanest thing to do with our now moment is to anticipate where we are going at the end of time, the destiny of our earthly life. We will ultimately come to the last moment of now. We don't know when it will be. Our Savior in the parables warns us to watch and pray because we do not know when death will come like a thief in the night. And that's why he counsels us to live every moment as though we were preparing for God to call us home.

Take some time to think of your now moment. Think of how old you are. Think of what has happened since your first memories of childhood. Think of how you have used the innumerable now moments of life. You may have used some of them very well. Others you may have wasted or used badly. But at the present moment, you are completely able to steer your now into eternity, no matter what you have done in the past. As St. Paul exclaimed, "See, now is the acceptable time; see, now is the day of salvation!" (2 Corinthians 6:2).

People addicted to destructive substances, even to drugs like codeine that put a steel band on the metabolism of their lives, have been known to change directions. I have known people who were slaves of drug addiction, who with the help of others went one day at a time into a better life. They were able to move from one now moment to the next by twelve-step programs. If a person can reject a severe narcotics habit, anyone can redirect his life with grace.

If you lack appreciation for the meaning of now, go and listen to some people tell their story at open Alcoholics Anonymous meetings, or perhaps participate in a parish retreat where people give witness talks about their conversion. Even simply reading stories of conversions can give you a great appreciation of the now.

The greatest danger is not the abuse of the now moment, because a person can be called to conversion. In the New Testament itself, people like St. Paul in a now moment turned around and went in a completely opposite direction. What is really dangerous is not so much a bad use of the present moment, but a lack of awareness of now—an unawareness of freedom, of self-direction, and of struggle. If a person does not recognize the importance of the present moment, his life will slip away like sand passing through an hour glass. And there will be nothing left. Rather, we must be like the apostles, who heard the Lord say "follow me" and who in a now moment abandoned everything and went after him.

—Fr. Benedict

For Reflection:

How can you use your now moment—today—to glorify God?

CHAPTER FOURTEEN

RANDOM ACTS OF KINDNESS

HINTS OF GOD'S GRACIOUSNESS

"I am the LORD, who exercises kindness, justice and righteousness on earth, for in these I delight," declares the LORD.
—JEREMIAH 9:24 (NIV)

Three things in human life are important. The first is to be kind. The second is to be kind. The third is to be kind.
—HENRY JAMES

A false popular opinion holds that the God of the Old Testament was more like a pagan god than the New Testament Father of Jesus. According to this view, he was harsh, even downright mean and arbitrary—just as apt to smite someone as to bless him. I think that people who believe this notion must not have read the Bible carefully. If they had, they would see that the God of both Testaments is characteristically kind.

The theme of God's unbounded kindness weaves through every page of Scripture. One of my favorite Old Testament passages says, "You are merciful to all, for you can do all things, and you overlook people's sins, so that they may repent" (Wisdom 11:23). And the New Testament commands us to be kind even to enemies, so that we can be like our heavenly Father: "For he makes his sun rise on the evil and on the good, and sends rain on the righteous and on the unrighteous" (Matthew 5:45). God was even kind to Cain, whom he had to punish for murdering his brother

Abel. When Cain said he feared that people would kill him, God put a mark on him in order to protect him from vengeance (see Genesis 4:15).

I have observed selfless acts of kindness in many saints and great Christians, which tells me that God has placed a hint of his own goodness in our human natures. And I have seen this divine quality in many people who are not yet saints, but whose compassionate behavior demonstrates our likeness to God.

First, let's look at saints, who consistently treated others kindly. I admire St. Fabiola (d. 399), a wealthy Roman matron and disciple of St. Jerome. She had divorced an abusive husband and married another man while her first husband was still alive, and so was excommunicated. Later she repaired her relationship with the church. Then she used her money to found the first hospital in the Western world. There she performed daily kindnesses for the sick. St. Jerome wrote,

> She often carried on her own shoulders persons infected with jaundice or covered with filth. She also often cleansed the revolting discharge of wounds, which others, even men, could not bear to look at. She fed her patients with her own hand, and moistened the scarce breathing lips of the dying with sips of liquid.[2]

Although St. Fabiola was not a nun, I like to think of her as a distant forebear of Mother Teresa.

Like Fabiola, St. Camillus de Lellis (1550–1614) lavished personal care on the sick. "I cannot get it out of my mind," said a companion, "that when he was attending a sick person, he looked like a hen with her chickens or like a mother at the bedside of her sick child."[3] Blessed Frederic Ozanam (1813–1853) in Paris and

Blessed Pier-Giorgio Frassati (1901–1925) in Turin spent themselves and their resources on personal compassionate care for the poor of their cities. The record of the kindnesses of the saints is endless, so I will stop listing them. But let me tell one more story about a "saint to be"[4] that has touched me deeply—the friendship between Bishop Fulton J. Sheen and Paul Scott.

During his senior year in high school, Paul Scott contracted leprosy. He spent the next six years lonely and frightened, confined to a leprosarium in Carville, Georgia. Newly discovered sulfone drugs halted Paul's disease, but not before he was disfigured beyond repair. His face had become an ugly mask, he was blind in one eye, he limped, and he had only partial use of his hands. Repelled by Paul's deformities, everyone, including friends and family, avoided him.

Depression and loneliness impelled Paul to look for help in an unlikely place. Although not a Catholic, he secured an appointment with Bishop Sheen, who had visited the facility in Carville and shown compassion to the patients. "I've come to you," said Paul, "because I have no one to turn to. I haven't a friend in the world."

"Well, now you have one," said the bishop.[5] Then Sheen supported Paul in practical ways. He helped the young man find and furnish an apartment. He provided him with clothes and food. He encouraged Paul to take a job behind the scenes in a social agency where his disfigurement would not be an impediment. Bishop Sheen even had Paul to dinner at his home once a week and, because Paul had difficulty using his hands, the bishop cut his food for him. And when Sheen was installed as Bishop of Rochester, New York, he had Paul seated in the cathedral's sanctuary as an honored guest. How's that for a reflection of God's kindness in a human being!

Many ordinary people—who certainly would not call themselves saints—are caught up in an informal movement that encourages acts of kindness. In 1993 American writer Anne Herbert published *Random Kindness and Senseless Acts of Beauty,*[6] the little book that has motivated tens of thousands to regularly surprise others with kindnesses. People committed to "random acts of kindness" often tell their stories on the Internet, and in them I see the marks of God's graciousness.[7] They "pay forward" for the tolls or fast food of people in line behind them. They regularly buy food for the homeless, give a stranded person a ride, or leave a flower or gift anonymously for someone grieving or otherwise having a hard time. Like the Creator, they continually invent new ways of treating others to unanticipated kindness.

The example of the saints and the "random kindness" folks prompt me to recognize a compassionate impulse in my heart. You may have the same reaction. Once we sense our God-inspired kindness, we must do something about it.

—BERT

For Reflection:

When have you experienced an unexpected kindness that made you aware of God?

CHAPTER FIFTEEN

FRESH STARTS

SIGNS OF GOD'S REDEMPTION

For you, O LORD, have delivered my soul from death,
my eyes from tears,
my feet from stumbling,
that I may walk before the LORD
in the land of the living.
—PSALM 116:8-9 (NIV)

Fr. Ed Thompson, associate pastor in my central Florida parish, is the best Bible-preaching priest I have ever heard.[8] His "Bible Blitzes"—guaranteed by a gigantic alarm clock to last only one hour—draw large crowds. In a hot July and August, five hundred parishioners came on Monday nights to hear him teach about the Gospel of John. He is also a very popular counselor and confessor. Involved in many ministries, he is so active at eighty-four that our retired bishop called him "the busiest priest in my diocese."[9]

Fr. Ed has not always been such a success. He is an alcoholic, and his addiction pushed him through a series of ups and downs until his drinking ended his pastoral work in 1991. "So long as you are under my authority," said the bishop of a western U.S. diocese, "you will never again serve as a practicing priest."[10]

But the story did not stop there. Fr. Ed believed that God wanted to restore him to the priesthood, and he prayed for that. Through a series of events that must be described as providential, God said yes to his prayer. Sober now for sixteen years, he has served fourteen of them as a much-appreciated priest in our parish. Fr. Ed's renewed life and ministry testify to God's desire, no matter how far we fall, to pick us up, wash off the dirt, and restore us to a place of honor in his kingdom. To me, Fr. Ed stands as a sacrament of God's redemptive grace, a sign of God's unquenchable desire to release us from whatever sin imprisons us. His story will jog your memory, causing you to recall fresh starts that God has prompted in your life and in the lives of those around you.

Fr. Ed says he did not start drinking until he was thirty-seven years old and in the ninth year of his priesthood. The night that John Kennedy was elected president in November 1960, he was celebrating with a bishop and four other priests. "Since we have our first Catholic president," said the bishop, "I think we should hoist one."[11] That one drink was all that it took to put Fr. Ed on his downward slide. He says he was like the man in the joke who ordered six consecutive shots of whiskey and drank only the last five. "Why didn't you drink the first one?" asks the bartender. "Because," says the man, "it's the first one that gets me drunk."[12] "I could never take just one drink," says Fr. Ed.

For thirty-one years Fr. Ed suffered with his addiction. A few sober years alternated with years when he was often drunk. Alcohol ruined all of his pastoral assignments. Several extended stays in treatment centers failed to cure him. Finally in 1991 his bishop, despairing that Fr. Ed would never be free of his addiction, sent him to a treatment center and suspended him from public service as a priest.

But Fr. Ed prayed, asking God to restore him to the active priesthood. And God responded by sending people to support him.

In the summer of 1991, Fr. Ed heard from a woman whom he had helped enter the Carmelite order thirty years before. Now married and divorced, she made contact with him. "You were the only one," she said, "who believed that Jesus communicated with me."[13] And when she sensed Jesus telling her that Fr. Ed was in trouble, she knew she had to help him. In July 1991, he left the treatment center and came to central Florida, and she welcomed him to live a short time in her home until he could afford a room on his own. She had four cats who became the congregation for his private Masses.

Shortly after arriving in Florida, Fr. Ed began to attend the 8:30 a.m. Mass in our parish, where he met the pastor, Fr. Paul Henry. One day Fr. Ed asked him to become his spiritual adviser. "I will be your friend," said Fr. Paul. He promised to pray for Fr. Ed and gradually involved him in parish ministries, arranging for him to teach in the adult education program and lead Bible studies. In November 1991, Fr. Ed attended the annual parish weekend retreat. On Sunday afternoon he sat in his car feeling physically, mentally, and spiritually spent. Crushed by the weight of his addiction, he shouted to God, pleading for release. Then he left the car and stood under a huge oak tree. Fr. Paul approached him and embraced him. In that moment of affection Fr. Ed says he had a spiritual awakening. He experienced all his resentment, anger, self-pity, and entitlement drain away. This new freedom helped him deal with the problems at the root of his alcoholism.

In August Fr. Ed had also started to attend Alcoholics Anonymous, which he had come to believe was his only hope for finally conquering his addiction. He had once heard Archbishop Fulton Sheen recommend that, if you wanted to find someone to give you good advice, you should look for a person who is suffering without complaint and trying to get close to God. Fr. Ed prayed for that kind of person to sponsor him in AA. He found such a man in Bob McCarthy, a sufferer seeking God, who had cancer of the throat and was worshipping at daily Mass. McCarthy agreed to sponsor Fr. Ed, but only on condition of absolute obedience.

"He put his finger in my face," says Fr. Ed, "and said, 'Disobey me once, and you're history.'"[14] For two years, McCarthy accompanied Fr. Ed to AA meetings two times and occasionally three times a day! His ministry to Fr. Ed. occasioned two redemptions: Fr. Ed has mastered his addiction for sixteen years running; and Bob McCarthy has been healed of his cancer, a mercy he attributes to his relationship with his priest friend.

Fr. Ed believed that God wanted to restore him to priestly ministry. He wrote his bishop in the western diocese, asking him to lift his suspension and allow him to function as a priest again. The bishop said no and declared that so long as he was his bishop, Fr. Ed would never serve as a priest again—unless another bishop was "crazy enough to accept him."[15]

Fr. Ed and Bob McCarthy prayed for his restoration. One day in 1993 at a novena to Our Lady, Bob predicted that Fr. Ed would celebrate Mass on her feast day. In the meantime, our local bishop, who appreciated Fr. Ed and his work, intervened on his behalf with his brother bishop out West and won the day. And Bob's prophetic insight came true: Fr. Ed was installed as a priest of our diocese on December 7, 1993 and celebrated Mass for the first time in our parish—the first public Mass of his restored priesthood—in honor of the Immaculate Conception on December 8.

Looking back now on his fresh start, Fr. Ed quotes his hero, Archbishop Fulton J. Sheen, who said, "Restored friendship is sweeter than unbroken love."[16]

—BERT

For Reflection:

In what area of your life do you need a fresh start? Ask someone you trust to support you in prayer for that new beginning.

CHAPTER SIXTEEN

LIGHT IN THE DARKNESS

BRINGING GOOD FROM EVIL

The light shines in the darkness,
and the darkness did not overcome it.

—JOHN 1:5

He did not spare his own Son, but gave him up
for the sake of all of us.

—ROMANS 8:32 (NJB)

I recently bumped into God in an unexpected place. Flipping through the pages of *Sports Illustrated,* I stopped to read Rick Reilly's column.[17] Reilly is an excellent writer, and I enjoy his insight and humor. This story was about the grace-filled response of Indianapolis Colts' coach Tony Dungy to his son's suicide. And in Reilly's account, I caught a glimpse of God doing one of his favorite things—bringing new life out of death.

Three days before Christmas 2005, eighteen-year-old James Dungy hanged himself from a ceiling fan in his Tampa Bay, Florida, apartment. Tony and Lauren, his wife, had no clue that their second oldest and outwardly easygoing child was troubled enough to take his own life. They still wonder why, but they do not expect an answer.

Like a good coach, Dungy took a hopeful approach to his grief: he looked forward, not backward, and focused on the next "game"—doing the next right thing. "It's human nature to grieve," he said, "and you're going to have some pain. But then the choice is how you handle the pain. You can choose to go on and fight through it, or you can choose to succumb to it. . . . It's hard to do, but that's what you have to do. You have to program yourself to live in the present. Make the present as good as you can make it."[18] Dungy went back to coaching after a week off. Just working with his men helped him deal with his loss.

"Family first" had always been Dungy's policy, but after James's death, he immediately renewed his commitment to spend time with his remaining five children. He shared about how as parents, we only have a few years with our children: "I guess what this whole thing has taught me is not to take that special time for granted. Really enjoy every day with them, make them feel like . . . they're really special."[19]

Impelled by his strong Christian faith, Dungy looked for other ways to bring good out of his family's tragic loss. In Rick Reilly's words, the celebrated football coach decided to become a coach for the grief stricken. The *Sports Illustrated* columnist described in detail how Dungy reached out to Mark Lemke, an Iowa truck driver. Mark's nineteen-year-old son, Cory, had recently died in a motorcycle accident.

One day Mark got an unusual phone call that he thought was a prank. "Mr. Lemke?" said the caller. "It's Tony Dungy." First Dungy had to assure Lemke that it was really him. Then he said, "I'm just calling to offer my condolences to you and see if there's anything I can do to help you."[20]

Thus began a friendship between two dads who were grieving the deaths of their sons. Right in the middle of the most important season of his career—aiming to take the Colts to the Super Bowl—Tony Dungy made a priority of communicating with Mark Lemke. "He takes the time to answer every Lemke e-mail, gives him his cell number and returns every call," said Reilly. "They go deep sometimes. Lemke gets hot at God for taking Cory. Dungy tells him that's normal, but he adds that if they keep their faith, 'we'll see them again.'"[21]

A few months later, Dungy led his Colts to the Super Bowl and made Lemke his honored guest at the big event. When they finally met in person, they hugged, visited, and prayed. "I'm awfully grateful to him," said Lemke. "He helped me keep my faith. He taught me that he and I—we're not alone."[22]

Mark Lemke is not the only beneficiary of Dungy's encouragement. He is bringing hope to many grief-stricken people. "I'll bet you," says Dungy, "I've talked to over two hundred people in the same situation. . . . On the one hand, it tells you you're not in this by yourself. There are a lot of people making it through. On the other hand, if you can share your feelings and say some things, it probably is going to help a lot of people."

In February 2006 at a Super Bowl breakfast—just two months after James died—Dungy reflected on the many blessings that he had witnessed following his son's death.[23] Two people who had received his son's corneas could now see. He had heard from many fathers who were deciding to pay more attention to their kids. Troubled teens told him that they were getting help. And he had learned that many people who witnessed his family's faith-filled response to James's death were giving their lives to the Lord.

Yet what if God has spoken to him in advance of his son's death and posed this question: "I can help some people see, I can repair some relationships, I can save some lives, and I can give some people eternal life, but I have to take your son to do it. You make the choice." Dungy then shook his head. "I would have said no, I'm sorry. I don't want to do that.

"But God had that choice and said yes. I'm going to do it. Two thousand years ago with his Son Jesus on the cross," said Dungy. "And because he made the choice I would not have made as a parent, he paved the way for us to come back into a relationship with him; he paved the way for us to see changed lives; and he let us know with certainty we can live with him in heaven."[24]

God specializes in bringing good out of evil. Or better, he replaces evil with good. That's the theme of God's own story that he told in the Bible. Scripture reports how God worked patiently over thousands of years to displace the evil forces that had usurped his creation. The story climaxed with his sending his only Son, Jesus, who launched the kingdom of God, a kingdom that would ultimately conquer the kingdom of darkness. By his death and resurrection, Jesus dealt all evil a death blow. Then he enlisted his followers to complete the job. He commissioned us to overcome the evil we find in our worlds and replace it with good—to shine Light into the darkness.

—BERT

For Reflection:

Recall a situation when you experienced God replacing evil with good. What was your response?

CHAPTER SEVENTEEN

FORGIVENESS

EVIDENCE OF GOD'S TOUCH

Bear with one another; forgive each other if one of you has a complaint against another. The Lord has forgiven you; now you must do the same.
—COLOSSIANS 3:13 (NJB)

If mercy were a sin, I believe I could not keep from committing it.
—ST. BERNARD OF CLAIRVAUX

Revenge comes easy to us. We chuckle at the bumper sticker that says, "I don't get mad. I get even." We like it because it expresses feelings that run deep in our disordered human natures. We often want to damage a person who damages us. When someone cuts us off in traffic, it's easier to wish him a flat tire than a blessing. Maybe even four flat tires.

But God says no to our desires for vengeance. "For my thoughts are not your thoughts," he says, "nor are your ways my ways" (Isaiah 55:8). And his thoughts and ways are rich in forgiveness (55:7), which he freely offers and prescribes for us as well. That's why Jesus required that we forgive those who trespass against us in the prayer he taught us and warned that if we did not forgive them, his Father would not forgive us (see Matthew 6:12, 14-15).

Okay. We can meet this requirement when the offense is trivial. God bless that nasty person who keyed the fender of my new car. But when the offense seems unbearably big, we wonder if we can manage to forgive. The angry faces of the parents of a murdered child stare at me from the pages of the local paper. They are demanding death for the killer. If someone were to take the life of one of mine, I ask myself, would I accept the grace to forgive him?

I find the example of Elisabeth Elliot both instructive and hopeful. In Ecuador in 1956, Stone Age tribesmen killed Jim Elliot, her husband, and four other missionaries. Elisabeth not only forgave Jim's killers, but she also reached out to them in love. Here's their story.[25]

Elisabeth had met Jim Elliot while studying at Wheaton College in Illinois in the late 1940s. She connected with him again while both were serving among the Quichua tribe in Ecuador. Elisabeth, a skilled linguist, was translating the New Testament into the Quichua language, and Jim was working to introduce Christianity to the tribe. They were married in Quito, Ecuador, in October 1953, and Valerie, their daughter, was born in February 1955.

In 1950 at a language institute, Jim had learned about the Aucas, a primitive tribe living in the jungles of Ecuador. From that moment, he became consumed with a passion to take the gospel to them. He seized every opportunity to survey the jungle by air, looking for Auca dwellings. He once wrote home, "We were looking for Auca homes, but found nothing. . . . More and more that tribe is brought before me as a field of labor for my life. . . . It would take a miracle to open the way to them, and we are praying for that miracle."[26]

In September 1955, word came from Nate Saint and Ed McCully, two other missionaries, that they had located an Auca settlement. Elisabeth says that from the instant the news arrived, Jim had one foot in the stirrup, ready to go. The men prayed more fervently for a chance to bring the good news to the Aucas. For five months, they made weekly flights over the Auca houses, dropping gifts of machetes, kettles, and ribbons and calling out greetings in the few Auca words they knew. By January 1956, they felt the time was right. Jim and four other men set up camp on the banks of the Curaray River near the Auca settlement. On January 8, the men flew over the Auca houses and invited the natives to meet them on the beach. They spotted ten Auca men heading toward their camp. They radioed their wives about the anticipated meeting. They were supposed to call back at 4:30 p.m. that day. The call never came. The men were found four days later, speared and scattered on the sand.

The story made big but brief news in the United States, including a spread in *Life* magazine. But the media did not cover the most significant part of the story. After dealing with her grief, Elisabeth forgave the men who had killed Jim. And she did it not only with heartfelt words but with actions. She decided that she would continue her husband's mission to take the good news to the Auca people, and she prayed for an opportunity to do so. She told a journalist, "The fact that Jesus Christ died for all makes me interested in the salvation of all, but the fact that Jim loved and died for the Aucas intensifies my love for them."[27]

Two years later, her prayers were answered. Three Auca women who lived among the Quichuas invited Elisabeth to come to the Auca settlement. In October 1958, Elisabeth, her daughter, and Rachel Saint, Nate's sister, moved to the village where her husband's killers lived. They stayed in a tiny open hut with hammocks for sleeping and an open pit for cooking. While the two women worked to translate the New Testament into the Auca language, they befriended the people, trying to teach them about God. Eventually a number of Aucas became Christian, including six of the men who had killed Jim and his companions. One of these men became pastor of the Auca church, and another was martyred himself when he tried to take the gospel to another Auca community.

At some point, Elisabeth was reconciled with the man who killed Jim. And as a sign of the reconciliation, he gave her his spear, which she keeps as a cherished memento in her home near Boston.[28]

I know the Christian teaching on forgiveness. I pray the Lord's Prayer often, forgiving those who have trespassed against me. But when someone offends me, I need something to prompt me to do it. I hope that in the heat of anger and pain, I remember Elisabeth's example and let God touch me with the grace to forgive.

—BERT

For Reflection:

Is there someone who has hurt you that you have not forgiven? Pray for God's grace to be able to do so.

CHAPTER EIGHTEEN

A CAUSE FOR HOPE

DIVINE PROVIDENCE

Life is not a simple product of laws and the randomness of matter, but within everything and at the same time above everything, there is a personal will, there is a Spirit who in Jesus has revealed himself as Love.
—POPE BENEDICT XVI[29]

As we make our way through life, with its happy moments and mishaps, with its joyous accomplishments and tragedies, we often wonder if this is all simply a random set of experiences. Is God rolling the dice with us? Obviously, mishaps, mistakes, and accidents happen. They can happen because of things wearing out, negligence, or ignorance. They can even result from the ill will or criminal desires of other people. And we are tempted to hold God responsible for the evils that befall us.

Faith gives a different explanation. It tells us that divine providence prepares us for the events of life, and it assures us that bad things do not come from God. St. Augustine said that God does not cause evil, but he causes the evil not to become the worst.

Christian faith tells us that by trusting in God and his providence, we can reverse the effects of whatever evil comes to us. The life of Christ demonstrates this truth most powerfully. The gospels ascribe the crucifixion of Jesus to the jealousy of the high priest, the betrayal of Judas, the weakness of Pilate, and ultimately to the devil himself, as when Luke writes that "Satan entered into Judas called Iscariot" (22:3).

But Jesus himself declared that he would triumph by reversing the enemy's evil. To Gentiles who approached him on the eve of his passion, he announced that his death would conquer the devil: "Now the ruler of this world will be driven out. And I, when I am lifted up from the earth, will draw all people to myself" (John 12:31-32). So Jesus clearly proclaimed the defeat of Satan. Thus, it is plain from the New Testament that the Lord is in the business of overcoming evil.

Both good things and bad things will occur in our lives. As we used to say in Jersey City, "We win some, we lose some, and some just get rained out." If we wish to grow in the Christian life, we must put all these matters into the hands of divine providence. We need to expect the Lord to bring good out of every evil.

But, we often want to ask, what about an infant born with severe deficiencies, or a person in their youth dying of a terminal illness, or disasters of nature like earthquakes, or wicked deeds like the destruction of the World Trade Center and the ensuing death of three thousand people? How can the Lord bring good out of such tragedies?

We can find one answer in the cross. I know women and men who transform evils that strike them by letting Jesus' crucifixion change their perspective. Like them, we can recognize that God himself became a man and endured the evil of a horrible death so that we could all enjoy the saving graces that came from the cross. And believing that the Lord destroyed the root of all evil on Calvary, we can look for the good that will come from the bad things that happen to us. Many families, for example, testify to the blessings they have received from caring for a child with disabilities. Others have softened their grief over an untimely death of a loved one—say, for example, from cancer—by working to raise funds for research to combat the disease or by volunteering to drive cancer patients to their doctor appointments.

Belief in eternal life also shows us how God brings good out of evil. Without belief in the afterlife promised by Christ, we might find human life unendurable. In the words of the old prayer, we would sorrow "as those who have no hope." Pope Benedict XVI, in his encyclical *Salve Spe,* has called us to live a life of hope. He extols the example of the African girl, St. Josephine Bakhita, who was enslaved at age nine and for thirteen years was treated brutally. Her master beat her daily, and later she was found to have 144 scars on her body. Finally, she was fortunate enough to be brought to Italy, where she met her true Master, and in 1896 became a Canossan sister. She never gave up hope. "I am definitely loved," she said, "and whatever happens to me—I am awaited by this Love."[30] And so the Lord raised her from her miserable circumstances and gave her the grace to become a saint. St. Paul said that we are saved by faith, but he also said that we are saved by hope (see Romans 8:24).

I have been deeply moved by the witness of a man who lived through the tragic loss of his beautiful family when desperados invaded his home and murdered his wife and children. Finding strength in his grief, with a firm confidence, he said quite simply at their funeral, "We must go on with hope." That man, speaking from the darkest sorrow and the most hideous injustice, gave witness to the very foundation of Christian belief that God reverses evils. As it did for this man, faith in divine providence, together with hope, enables us to go on. Even if we do not come to a full resolution of the tragic situations in our lives, our struggles, faith, and hope will create grace-filled opportunities for others to change things in the future.

—FR. BENEDICT

For Reflection:

Think back to one situation when you trusted God in a difficult circumstance. How did your faith and hope help you?

Questions for Group Discussion

1. Why do you think it is important to pay attention to the "now" moment?

2. How do you benefit from performing acts of kindness?

3. When has God given a second chance to you or to someone close to you?

4. When have you witnessed God bringing good out of evil? How did it build your faith?

5. How do you think our forgiving someone for an offense compares to God's forgiving us? What is the difference?

6. What is your reaction when bad things happen to you? Do you think you rely enough on God to get you through them?

Part Four

REAL PRESENCE

CHAPTER NINETEEN

REVELATION

GOD TAKES THE INITIATIVE

What did Jesus actually bring? . . . The answer is very simple: God.
He has brought God. He has brought God who formerly unveiled
his countenance gradually, first to Abraham, then to Moses and the
Prophets, and then in the Wisdom literature. . . . He has brought God,
and now we know his face, now we can call upon him. Now we know
the path that we human beings have to take in this world.

—POPE BENEDICT XVI[1]

When you consider the history of religion in general, particularly the history of the Jewish faith, and finally the history of Christianity, one thing becomes obvious: God wants to communicate with his children. We have learned that without that communication, we would be blindly making our way through a difficult world. We know that if God had not taken the initiative to reveal himself to us, we would have no hope of salvation.

We have already reflected on God's revelation of himself in the material world. All creation shimmers with his presence. His marvelous handiwork declares his desire to relate to his human creatures. Without a word, trillions of stars, birds, animals, fish, and plants announce his closeness to us. And scientists who observe the invisible micro world of atoms, viruses, and genes tell us that they see and hear God in the specimens that they study. For example, eminent biologist Francis S. Collins spoke of God's self-revelation in an article on CNN's Web site:

As the director of the Human Genome Project, I have led a consortium of scientists to read out the 3.1 billion letters of the human genome, our own DNA instruction book. As a believer, I see DNA, the information molecule of all living things, as God's language, and the elegance and complexity of our own bodies and the rest of nature as a reflection of God's plan.[2]

When natural disasters such as hurricanes, tornadoes, and floods occur, the material world even appears to be in rebellion against God. But we know that God can bring good out of these evils. For instance, we see the evidence of grace in the human community when it rallies to aid the victims of such catastrophes. However, most of the time, the natural world is generous and fecund. Its bounty provides the vast majority of people more than enough to eat, and if things were properly distributed, there would be no hunger.

Beyond revealing himself in the material world, God has communicated with us more directly in sacred Scripture. From Genesis, the first book of the Old Testament, to Revelation, the last book of the New Testament, the Bible communicates God's thoughts and words to human beings. He called Abraham to leave his homeland and promised to establish him as the father of a great nation (see Genesis 12:1-2). He chose to reveal himself to the Hebrews, an obscure nomadic tribe. He spoke to Moses from the burning bush, revealing his name as "I AM WHO I AM," the source and sustainer of all being (see Exodus 3:1-5, 13). And he gradually unfolded his plan of salvation through the prophets, promising in David a future king who would reign forever (see 1 Kings 2:45; Isaiah 9:7).

And ultimately he has come to us by his only Son. Our Lord Jesus Christ is called the Word of God because he is God's revelation to us. The opening verse of the Gospel of John—"In the beginning was the Word, and the Word was with God, and the Word was God"—shows the intimate and necessary connection between creation and God's speaking to us. If you look at reality, from the vast multitude of stars down to the complexity of the atomic world, you can say that God made all of this so that he could reveal himself to human beings. He created everything just so that he could communicate with us, not only as a race, but as individuals, so that we might know, love, and serve him and come to eternal salvation.

As Christians we should be most receptive to the word of God. We should read all of Scripture with the greatest care and respect. We especially revere the New Testament because it contains the words and actions of our Lord Jesus Christ. When these words were written about the life of Christ, no one had a tape recorder, and no one was on the scene with a video camera. But when we hear the voice of God in the gospels, we are hearing the preaching of the apostolic church. We are listening to what Peter and Paul, our mother Mary, the holy women who gathered at the cross, and the disciples at Pentecost remembered about the teaching and life of Jesus.

If you compare the serious and respected ancient religions, including Buddhism, Hinduism, and even what we know of the traditional African and Asian religions, with the revealed religion of the Bible, you will see that in Christianity, a whole new picture of God emerges. That picture is most clearly defined by the face of our Lord Jesus Christ. The New Testament, especially the gospels, presents the face of the living God in Christ. We should take every opportunity to know that face and to listen to the initiative that God has taken in our regard.

We must always approach Scripture with faith. That is where we start. We believe that the carpenter from Nazareth, a remote village in a militarily occupied land, was in fact the eternal Son of God who took upon himself a true human body and soul in the womb of the Virgin Mary.

—FR. BENEDICT

For Reflection:

Why do you think God progressively revealed himself to humankind until he finally revealed himself fully in Jesus?

CHAPTER TWENTY

THE LIVING WORD

FINDING GOD IN SCRIPTURE

As the rain and the snow come down from heaven,
and do not return to it without watering the earth
and making it bud and flourish,
so that it yields seed for the sower and bread for the eater,
so is my word that goes out from my mouth:
It will not return to me empty,
but will accomplish what I desire and achieve the purpose
for which I sent it.

—ISAIAH 55:10-11 (NIV)

I am a voracious reader, and I devour many different kinds of books. For my work as an editor, I read books about Scripture, prayer, sacraments, testimony, and theology. For relaxation, I read biographies, histories, thrillers, and mystery fiction. Among my many favorite authors, I especially enjoy C. S. Lewis and F. J. Sheed. Now and then, they write something that I don't understand or agree with, and I wish I could talk to them about it. But, of course, I cannot, because they are dead.

As a matter of fact, even when I am reading books by authors who are still alive, they really are "dead" to me. I cannot ask novelist Michael Connelly a question about a plot in a mystery or argue a point with New Testament scholar N. T. Wright and expect either of them to answer me. Okay, you savvy readers may advise me to check out their Web sites or e-mail them. But my point is that when we are sitting in our easy chairs and reading their books, all authors are technically dead to us because we cannot converse with them directly, at that very moment. Just try talking to me about this book—as far as you're concerned, I'm dead, and I won't speak with you from these pages.

However, there is one exception: the Author of the Bible. He is not "dead" to us but very much alive in its pages. God himself truly dwells in the books of Scripture. Our Jewish brothers and sisters recognized this fact; they experience him being just as fully present to them in the Torah, the first five books of the Bible, as their ancestors experienced him in the Temple. Christians in the Eastern churches revere the Lord's real presence in the Bible and store it along with the Eucharist in the tabernacle.

So when we read Scripture, we can pause over a sentence and ask the divine Author to help us figure out its meaning. We can expect the Lord to lead us to an answer, or we can just anticipate that through his words, he will touch our lives in some way.

We can see many examples of the way the word of God in Scripture has transformed lives. The Ethiopian eunuch was reading Isaiah's prophecy of the crucifixion when Philip came to him and interpreted the passage for him. The living word converted him to Christ, Philip baptized him, and he went on his way rejoicing (Acts 8:26-39). Anthony of Egypt (c. 251–356), the heir to wealthy landowners, changed his life when he heard this gospel command: "If you wish to be perfect, go, sell your possessions, and give the money to the poor . . . then come, follow me" (Matthew 19:21). For the next eighty years, this saint lived a life of prayer and penitence as a hermit.[3]

The word of God touched and won St. Augustine (354–430) when he read these sentences from Romans: "Let us conduct ourselves becomingly as in the day, not in reveling and drunkenness, not in debauchery and licentiousness, not in quarreling and jealousy. But put on the Lord Jesus Christ, and make no provision for the flesh, to gratify its desires" (see 13:13-14).[4] And St. Francis of Assisi (1181–1226) converted when these words from the Gospel of Matthew stabbed him with conviction:[5]

> And as you go, proclaim that the kingdom of Heaven is close at hand. Cure the sick, raise the dead, cleanse those suffering from virulent skin-diseases, drive out devils. You received without charge, give without charge. Provide yourselves with no gold or silver, not even with coppers for your purses, with no haversack for the journey or spare tunic or footwear or a staff, for the laborer deserves his keep. (10:7-10, NJB)

Over the centuries, as Luke said in the Book of Acts, "The word of the Lord spread widely and grew in power" (19:20, NIV). Many people in your social environments could tell you how God's presence in the Bible has impacted their lives. Let me tell you one contemporary story about how an encounter with God's living word transformed a young man's life.[6]

One year, shortly after Easter, Anthony Cassano visited a lay Christian community and stayed in their guest house. His hosts, a young couple and four other community members, seemed to have little in common, humanly speaking. But Anthony detected a spiritual unity among them that intrigued him. He had grave doubts about the existence of God, so he was especially fascinated by his hosts' conversations. "They talked about Jesus," he said, "as someone who played an important role in their lives. They talked about him as someone they had met. This floored me."[7]

Anthony joined the household for afternoon prayers, but he did not pray himself, because he did not believe there was anyone to pray to. For several days, he sat through their prayer gatherings as a neutral observer. But one afternoon, the Easter antiphon that opened and closed the prayer time touched his heart:

> When it was evening on that day, the first day of the week, and the doors of the house where the disciples had met were locked. . . . Jesus came and stood among them and said, "Peace be with you." (John 20:19)

That verse about the resurrection struck him, and he thought, "*This* afternoon, in *this* house, in *this* motley group being gathered together in *this* living room, the same event is repeating itself. Jesus is here."[8] The awareness of the Lord's presence made known through that Scripture passage led Anthony to take his first steps toward God. And now, years later, he says that same verse frequently reminds him of the presence of Jesus who, in conquering death, brings us his peace.

Isaiah had it right. God's word is alive and active, and it does exactly what he sends it to do.

—BERT

For Reflection:

Recall an occasion when a Scripture passage made you aware of God's presence. What disposition or attitude in prayer helped you become aware of God speaking to you?

CHAPTER TWENTY-ONE

JESUS

REVEALING THE NATURE OF GOD

Whoever has seen me has seen the Father.
—JOHN 14:9

It's all because of Jesus that we speak of God as we do.
—N. T. WRIGHT[9]

When the whole Ghezzi clan gathers for a holiday event, we number twenty-seven, including sons, daughters, spouses, and grandchildren—a lovely and active flock. And when I survey the scene, I can see that I have left my mark on all of my seven adult children.

On the negative side, some of them have inherited my compulsion to control things. Some share my feisty temper. Some imitate my perverse sense of humor. On the positive side, like me, all the kids are quick to serve when they see a need. In particular, John, my oldest, exercises a fatherly concern for his siblings. He calls or e-mails them frequently and offers support, advice, and encouragement.

Just by living with us, our children take on some of our characteristics. People see something of us in our sons and daughters, because in their person and behaviors they reveal our natures.

Analogously, Jesus revealed the nature of God in his words and actions. The fact is that if it were not for Jesus, we would not know much about God the Father or God the Holy Spirit.

Without his witness, we would not have a clue about the Trinity. As wonderful as our reason is, we could never have figured out on our own that God is three Persons in one divine nature—that God is one in three and three in one.

At the Last Supper, Jesus summed up his revelations about God. In his final conversations with his disciples, he spoke about the unity of the Father, Son, and Spirit that the church would later recognize as the Trinity. For example, when Philip asked Jesus to make the Father known, he responded with surprise:

> "Have I been with you all this time, Philip, and you still do not know me? Whoever has seen me has seen the Father. How can you say, 'Show us the Father'? Do you not believe that I am in the Father and the Father is in me? The words that I say to you I do not speak on my own; but the Father who dwells in me does his works." (John 14:9-10)

From the outset of his public ministry, Jesus announced that his Father was at work in his person, establishing the kingdom of God at the expense of the kingdom of darkness. He demonstrated his Father's plan to rescue humanity from sin and sickness by his miracles of healing and deliverance. When Jewish leaders criticized him for healing a paralytic on the Sabbath, he responded, "My Father is still working, and I also am working" (John 5:17). Then he further explained his collaboration with the Father in bringing new life to humanity:

> "Very truly, I tell you, the Son can do nothing on his own, but only what he sees the Father doing; for whatever the Father does, the Son does likewise. The Father loves the Son and shows him all that he himself is doing; and he will

show him greater works than these, so that you will be astonished. Indeed, just as the Father raises the dead and gives them life, so also the Son gives life to whomever he wishes." (John 5:19-21)

Also, at the Last Supper, Jesus described in some detail the role of the Holy Spirit. He promised that the Spirit would come to his followers as the Advocate to support them (John 14:16-17). Then he revealed the mysterious truth that for those who loved and obeyed him, he and the Father would come and make their home in them (14:23). Christians would later come to understand that the presence of the Father and the Son within us is a primary work of the Spirit. And as Jesus had assured the disciples, it was the Holy Spirit who accomplished this marvelous work and taught us about it (see 14:26; Acts 1:4-5; 2:4).

Such reflections lead me to conclude that if we want to know what God is like, we should study Jesus. New Testament scholar N. T. Wright says that by looking hard at Jesus, especially on his way to his death, we will learn more about God than by gazing at the wonders of nature or by reflecting on the moral law.[10] So let's consider the qualities of God that we can see in Jesus at his passion and death. Looking at Jesus in his last fifteen hours before death, we learn that God is

—Patient. Just as Jesus showed patience at Gethsemane with the disciples who could not stay awake to pray (Matthew 26:42-45), God is patient with us, giving us time to repent of sins and return to him (see Wisdom 11:21–12:2).

—Meek. Meekness is strength under control, and Jesus walked through the terrible events leading up to his crucifixion in complete control of himself and the situation. Likewise, no matter what happens in our lives, God deals with us with divine meekness—that is, with his divine strength, he keeps things under control.

—Merciful. Racked with pain, Jesus looked down from the cross and asked his Father to forgive those who had crucified him.

—Kind. Just as Jesus kindly welcomed the good thief into paradise and asked the Beloved Disciple to care for Mary, God's kindness constantly envelops us (see Psalm 23:6).

—Humble. We may think that humility is appropriate only for human beings before God. But God, in Christ, humbly submitted to a shameful death in order to serve all human beings (see Philippians 2:8).

And in Christ Jesus, whose whole life was one great act of love that climaxed in his complete gift of self in the crucifixion, we see the fullest expression of the nature of God, who is love (see 1 John 4:8).

—BERT

For Reflection:

What is it about Jesus that most reveals God to you?

CHAPTER TWENTY-TWO

THE REAL WORLD

THEOLOGY AND THE LOVE OF GOD

Sanity, remember, does not mean living in the same world as everyone else; it means living in the real world. But some of the most important elements in the real world can only be known by the revelation of God, which it is theology's business to study.
—FRANK J. SHEED[11]

At first light this morning, I left the quiet darkness of my house and walked out to the front yard. Blackbirds crowed, alerting each other that I was nearby. The already humid Florida air clung to me, and I smelled the musky odor of fresh-cut grass blended with the perfume of my neighbor's gardenias. I waved at a man and woman who were walking their golden retriever. I picked up the morning paper from the driveway. I examined my new crape myrtle and noticed dewdrops sparkling on its leaves. The moon was still visible in the cloudless morning sky. I was in touch with the "real" world—or was I?

In his classic book *Theology and Sanity*, Frank J. Sheed warns that in spite of what our senses tell us, we may not be fully aware of reality. He says that vast, important parts of the real world are spiritual and invisible. So our senses give us only a very limited perception of what's real. Sheed says further that if we restrict ourselves to a purely material view of things, we remain out of touch with reality and, therefore, are technically insane. Sanity, after all, means living in the real world, and it contains elements that we can know only by God's revelation. That's where theology comes in. It helps us grasp the truths that are essential to our sanity. Sheed says these realities include

> God, infinite and eternal, Trinity, Unity; humanity, created in time, fallen and redeemed by Christ; the individual human person born into the life of nature, reborn into the life of grace, united by Christ in the Church which is His Mystical Body, aided by angels, hindered by devils, destined for heaven, in peril of hell.[12]

If what Sheed says is true, and I believe it is, then consideration of such realities and reflecting on them is indispensable to our well-being. We must pursue at least a minimal understanding of theology, but the more we pursue it, the better off we will be.

Studying theology provides food for our minds.[13] In his confrontation with the devil, Jesus said that we do not "live by bread alone, but by every word that comes from the mouth of God" (Matthew 4:4; see Deuteronomy 8:3). Knowing, for example, that God created me from nothing and that he sustains me in being grounds me in reality and establishes my mental health. Otherwise, I live in the fantasy that I exist on my own and can do whatever I want without any accountability. But think about it. Before I became someone, I was nothing at all, and without Someone holding me in being, back to nothing I would go. That's real food for thought.[14]

The study of theology is also food for our hearts. The more we know about God, the more we have reason to love him. This morning at Mass, for example, the first reading from Genesis told of Abraham's willingness to sacrifice Isaac, his only son (see chapter 22). I was deeply moved by the reading and by the priest's explanation of its theological significance. He reflected on God's willingness, out of his great love, to give his only Son as a sacrifice for the redemption of all humanity—including me. Meditating on this theological truth easily flows into greater love of God. I left Mass feeling that I had received nourishment for my heart.

Throughout the course of history, theological truths have penetrated leaden hearts and turned people to God. For example, consider an event in the life of St. Dominic (1170–1221). In 1203 Dominic accompanied his bishop on a diplomatic mission from Osma, Spain, to Denmark. Their journey took them through Languedoc in southern France, which was a stronghold of Albigensian heretics.

Albigensianism proclaimed a strict dualism, holding that everything material is evil and everything spiritual is good. So these heretics challenged core Christian doctrines. They denied the humanity of Christ because they believed that a wicked body could not contain God's pure spirit. Therefore, they held that Jesus did not suffer, die, and rise again, and that his redemptive work consisted in releasing good human spirits from captivity in wicked bodies. Because anything bodily was evil, they rejected the sacraments and the resurrection of the body. [15]

The diplomatic party stopped at Toulouse, and Dominic stayed at an inn with an Albigensian host. He spent the night debating theology with the man in order to persuade him that his views were false. The record does not provide details about their discussion. But we can speculate with some confidence that Dominic presented convincing arguments about such doctrines as creation, the incarnation, redemption, and the resurrection of the body. By morning Dominic and theological truth had prevailed. The innkeeper renounced the heresies and embraced authentic Christianity.[16] This success set the course for Dominic's preaching ministry, which used theology to win the minds and hearts of Albigensians in northern Italy and southern France.

We must study theology not only for our own sanity but also for the spiritual health of many of our neighbors who, says Sheed, are living "a half-blind life, trying to cope with a reality most of which [they] do not know is there."[17] We must share with them the food for the mind and heart that we find in our own reflections on doctrine.

—BERT

For Reflection:

How has your consideration of a doctrine increased your love of God?

CHAPTER TWENTY-THREE

THE EUCHARIST

MEETING GOD IN THE LITURGY

While they were eating, Jesus took a loaf of bread, and after blessing it he broke it, gave it to the disciples, and said, "Take, eat; this is my body." Then he took a cup, and after giving thanks he gave it to them, saying, "Drink from it, all of you; for this is my blood of the [new] covenant, which is poured out for many for the forgiveness of sins."
—MATTHEW 26:26-28

*Mary conceived Christ in her womb
and we bear him about in our heart.*

—ST. PETER DAMIAN

When Jesus appeared on the scene in Galilee, he immediately announced the arrival of God's kingdom. God was acting through him to rescue women and men from the kingdom of darkness. In Jewish culture, eating together was an expression of friendship, and Jesus demonstrated his love and friendship by sharing meals with these men and women. He frequently attended dinner parties at the homes of public sinners and reclined at table with disreputable tax collectors, prostitutes, thieves, and other commandment breakers.

This alarmed the Pharisees, who believed that strict observance of the law required Jews to shun evildoers. When they challenged him, Jesus explained that he had come to befriend sinners and to bring them healing, forgiveness, and new life.

But Jesus had not come just for sinners who were his contemporaries. He came to liberate and bring new life to all sinners—past, present, and future. He had to do something extraordinary, something that would penetrate the limits of time and space of his passion, death, and resurrection. Given Jesus' practice of dining with sinners, we should not be surprised, then, that the vehicle he chose for this saving work was a special meal.

The night before he died, Jesus and his disciples dined together for the last time. They celebrated the Passover supper, which re-presented the deliverance of the Jews from Egypt. While they were at table, Jesus fed them with the Eucharist, that sacramental meal that re-presents his crucifixion, which delivered us from our sin and death. He changed bread into his body and wine into his blood, and gave them to us as food to nourish our spirits. So he arranged that he would always be really present to us as we carried him in our hearts. Over the years, millions of Christians have met the Lord personally in this sacrament. And through devotion to Christ in the Eucharist, many have experienced his love in ways that transformed their lives. Consider just one example in the story of Bill Wingard, Jr.[18]

When Bill's mother died while he was in first grade, he felt "stunned, saddened, and confused." He adds, "I had this feeling of being alone, as if I had been abandoned—and it wouldn't go away. Yes, my father was there. Yes, I knew that he loved me, but a big chunk of me was missing."[19]

One day his class gathered in the school chapel for Eucharistic adoration. Bill and his friends sat or knelt, fidgeting a little, before the golden monstrance, which contained the host that the priest held up at Mass. The nuns had explained that this was actually Jesus' body, and Bill was impressed. Then something Bill never expected happened that would heal his sense of loss:

In that little chapel an awareness of warmth and happiness came over me, and I sensed that God wanted to tell me something that would get to the real hurt deep inside me. With a voice that was at once awesomely quiet yet very clear, God spoke to me in the solitude of my mind and heart: "I will never abandon you. You are special to me." At once that intense loneliness went away, and in its place was a joy deeper than words could describe. This was the beginning of my lifelong love affair with Jesus in the Eucharist.[20]

This kind of devotion to Christ in the Eucharist holds a significant place in Christian spirituality. But we must also see personal Eucharistic piety in the context of a much bigger picture. For the Lord changes bread and wine into his body and blood not just for Bill or you or me. He becomes present in the Eucharist for the spiritual life of the whole church.

Here's the point: Scripture teaches that the church is the body of Christ (see 1 Corinthians 12:12-30; Ephesians 4:11-16). Christ's divine life flows through the body from him as the head to all the members. And the Eucharist as "the source and summit of the Christian life"[21] nourishes the body and strengthens it to continue Christ's work of restoring people to his Father's kingdom. So all the church's worship—all the sacraments and the Liturgy of the Hours—and all the church's ministries and outreaches, are connected to the Eucharist. As the *Catechism of the Catholic Church* puts it, "In the blessed Eucharist is contained the whole spiritual good of the Church, namely Christ himself."[22]

We can see this reality illustrated in the lives of the saints. For example, consider the practice of Dorothy Day, the cofounder of the Catholic Worker movement and now a candidate for canonization. She regarded all the service she and her colleagues did for the poor as rooted in the Eucharist. It was Christ present in them who reached out to the sick, the drunks, and the addicts that they met on the streets and cared for with love. And when Dorothy Day prayed the Liturgy of the Hours—an extension of the Eucharist that consecrated her days—she knew that she was joining the prayer of Christ himself. "Living the liturgical day as much as we are able," she wrote, "beginning with prime, using the missal [at Mass], ending the day with compline and so going through the liturgical year we find that it is now not us, but Christ in us, who is working to combat injustice and oppression."[23]

Through the Mass and the Liturgy of the Hours, Jesus himself strengthened Dorothy and her associates for their difficult and sometimes thankless service. So at Christ's invitation, we approach the Eucharist with expectation. We take and eat his body and drink his blood so that we might love him more personally and so that under his lead, we might carry on our part of his work.

—BERT

For Reflection:

In what ways have I met Jesus in the Eucharist? How have I experienced his strengthening me for my Christian service?

CHAPTER TWENTY-FOUR

MIRACLES

They brought to him all the sick, those who were afflicted
with various diseases and pains, demoniacs, epileptics, and paralytics,
and he cured them.

—MATTHEW 4:24

God's presence in the world often leads to wonderful events that awaken us to divine power going beyond the observable laws of nature. We use the word "miracle," which can have several different but related meanings, to describe these inexplicable events. There are medical miracles and miracles officially recognized by the church.

I am an example of a medical miracle. There is no reason at all why I'm able to write these words. Four years before this book was written, I was a victim of a serious traffic accident. As a result, I was in a state equivalent to physical death for twenty-seven minutes. I had no vital signs. I had no blood pressure, no heartbeat, and no respiration. I was dead. Realizing that all these readings were flat, after fifteen minutes the doctors were going to give up on me. The young priest with me begged them to go on. They told him that if I revived, I would be a vegetable. It was absolutely clear to the medical personnel that if I lived, I would never think, I would never walk. But I did revive, and I do both!

However, I am not an official church miracle. The church requires that for something to be called a miraculous cure, it must occur instantaneously or very rapidly without any recovery period. That's what the medical bureau at Lourdes requires to verify a miracle. And the Congregation for the Causes of Saints, the Vatican office responsible for the canonization process, also insists on the same strict criteria for miracles worked through the intercession of candidates for sainthood.

Especially in our scientific age, many find it hard to deal with events that can't be explained logically. Mysteries and miracles can be quite unsettling to skeptics, who might prefer to avoid the issue altogether. About such doubters, Albert Einstein, arguably the greatest scientist who ever lived, once said that people who could not react with wonder and awe to the mysteries of life might as well be dead. He was a great believer in the mysterious and miracles, and particularly liked to discuss the mystery of the Eucharist with priests.

There is a great deal of prejudice against the idea of the *supernatural*, as if human beings really understood the idea of the *natural* realm. If someone says to you, "There is no supernatural," ask him to define the meaning of the natural. He will have a difficult time and probably will attribute various things to "Mother Nature." Just ask him where that lady lives. Where did she come from? And what is she doing? In fact, the term "nature" is really an illusionary construction of the mind that often helps us avoid dealing with the real mysteries of life. Science itself is filled with mysteries—the nature of life, time, matter, gravity, and more. Miracles bring into the discussion interventions of God's power that do not follow the ordinary observable laws of nature.

The Catholic Church is not bashful about miracles. It will carefully examine and even identify a few. But only a few. For example, out of tens of thousands of cures reported at Lourdes, fewer than seventy healings have ever been declared as airtight cases and recognized as miracles. But the church encourages us to accept medical miracles as evidences of God's loving action in the world. Let me share two examples.

Dr. Alexis Carrel, a Nobel Prize winner and director of the most prestigious scientific agency of his time, observed and described a first-class miracle of healing at Lourdes. He was there. He watched as a young woman in a few moments came back to life from the doors of death. Awestruck at the sight of the woman's recovery, Carrel declared, "It was the resurrection of the dead; it was a miracle!" I have reported Dr. Carrel's account of his experience in my book *The Journey Toward God*.[24]

I was privileged as a young Capuchin novice to live with Fr. Solanus Casey for almost a year. I often served Mass for him. I observed him closely and saw him one night lost in ecstasy before the tabernacle at two o'clock in the morning. I was a witness in the cause for his beatification as a saint. For forty years, Solanus served as a doorkeeper at monasteries in New York and Detroit. Thousands of people came to him for counsel and healing. He turned no one away and prayed for all. At the time of his death, his Capuchin province had on file reports of nine hundred miracles attributed to his prayers. The record is astounding: cancer patients, babies with incurable diseases, the mentally ill—you name it—all were healed through the intercession of this humble priest. Many of these miracles were attested to medically by physicians and at least one by the Mayo Clinic.

It is not the job of doctors or clinics to identify a miracle. It is their responsibility, however, at times to say that there is no medical explanation for what is going on. In discussing the case of a reported miracle in the cause of the beatification of Cardinal Terrence Cooke, I asked the physician who had attended a girl dying of leukemia what he thought. She had been very close to death. Her entire parish had prayed for her recovery through Cardinal Cooke's intercession. Her leukemia disappeared in one hour, and it never returned. The physician, a devout Jewish man, said to me, "I don't know about miracles. I'm a doctor, but I'll tell you this: the hand of the Almighty was there."

The hand of the Almighty is mighty indeed. So when we witness or hear about a miraculous cure, we should kneel down and give thanks for the privilege of having experienced God's loving intervention.

—FR. BENEDICT

For Reflection:

When have you observed God intervening in someone's life? How did it affect your faith?

QUESTIONS FOR GROUP DISCUSSION

1. In what sense do you think that the New Testament presents the face of Christ?

2. Why should you pray to the Holy Spirit before reading Scripture?

3. What has reflecting on Jesus taught you about God the Father?

4. Why do you think reflecting on a doctrine can increase your love of God? Explain with an example.

5. How does the sacrament of the Eucharist strengthen the life of the whole church?

6. When have you witnessed someone's conversion? Would you call God's action in this case a miracle?

Part Five

COMMUNICATION WITH GOD

CHAPTER TWENTY-FIVE

LISTENING TO LIFE

GOD SPEAKS IN EVERY MOMENT

*The voice of God, having once penetrated the heart, becomes strong as
the tempest and loud as the thunder. But before reaching the heart it is as
weak as a light breath that scarcely agitates the air. It shrinks from noise
and is silent amid agitation.*

—ST. IGNATIUS OF LOYOLA

I hope by now that Bert and I have convinced you that God is continually speaking to you in everyday events. And I hope we have
persuaded you to listen to him in your present moments.

If you want to hear what God is saying to you, you must learn
to listen to life, that multifaceted flow of events that fills the passing of your time. That may be simple, but it's not easy because
life comes at you fast. So many things are happening around you
that you can pay attention only to the few that catch your attention. You can't be listening to all conceivable distractions along
the way, because their velocity and volume will drown out the
voice of God. But as you master the art of listening to life, you
will come to hear the Lord speaking in your mind and heart.

Listening to life involves a form of selective hearing. We turn a
deaf ear to the many sounds that constantly bombard us—a tick-
ing clock, the whirring of a fan, the burbling of a dishwasher, the
din of traffic. Listening is a matter of responding to what we hear.
And listening to life in order to hear God's voice means responding

with our mind and heart. Consider this example that I described in my book *Listening at Prayer:*[1]

> We hear a disturbed person muttering to himself on a busy street corner, and if we notice at all we say, "He should be hospitalized." The person of prayer [who listens to life] hears the muttering voice and more, because within he hears the "cry of the poor"[2] and in that he hears the voice of the Son of God. The prayerful person responds with some gesture of kindness, some help, or if nothing else can be done, with a prayer bringing the sufferer before God.

As we listen to life, we recognize the voice of the Lord in occurrences in the material world, in books, in music, in Scripture, in the liturgy, and in people we meet. Could you not have heard God speaking in the famous news account of the mother hen found burnt to a crisp in a California forest fire? The covering of her blackened wings had saved the lives of her chicks. Personally, I enjoy listening to God in music—in great choirs singing classical hymns or Gregorian chant. Another form of "listening" that I enjoy is to watch the people I encounter, especially when traveling on the subway or walking along a sidewalk in Manhattan. Many look lonely or sad, and my heart goes out to them. Like Thomas Merton, who once was overwhelmed with love for people he met on a Louisville, Kentucky, street, I wish I could tell them "that they are all walking around shining like the sun."[3]

Listening to life in the present moment requires that we divest ourselves as far as possible of our preconceived expectations. We must become like the simple souls we know who just take life as it comes.

In recent years, as I have let go of certain expectations, I've been discovering new things about myself and my life. Ever since I was struck by a car in a very serious accident, I've had to learn to listen to my body. Before that time, I was not accustomed to paying much attention to my body. But now I have to listen to my limitations and my handicaps and let them say something to me. Sometimes when I wake up in the morning, I start to feel the pains of the day, and I say, "What in the world is this? How am I going to put up with this? Why did God let this happen to me?" Then I have to rewind the tape, so to speak, and ask, "What are my pains and aches telling me?" I am learning to respond with mind and heart to what they are saying.

They tell me a number of good things, which I think come from God. First of all, they remind me that our life here doesn't last forever, and that everyone, even the healthiest person, is not going to be here for a very long time. Secondly, my pains tell me to be compassionate to others in pain, especially to the disabled. Now that I am somewhat disabled myself, I realize how little I had understood about what it's like to be physically challenged. And when I think of someone who is blind or someone who has never walked a step in his life, I cannot even consider my handicaps very serious. My pains and limitations give me insight into what many people in the world have to suffer.

So God is communicating with us in the flow of events in our lives. He may be telling us to be patient, to be brave, to be courageous, to be kind, to be understanding, or to be forgiving. Whatever happens—even something sad and tragic—can send a message to us.

In a serious moment, comedienne Gracie Allen once said, "Never put a period where God has put a comma." Her wit may make you smile, but it sums up an important truth: if we want to hear what God is saying to us, we must keep on listening to life.

—FR. BENEDICT

For Reflection:

In which recent event is God saying something to you?

CHAPTER TWENTY-SIX

PRAYER

OPENING TO GOD

Prayer is essentially a dialogic encounter between God and man; and since God is the Lord, he alone can initiate the encounter. . . . What man does or says in prayer will depend on what God does or says first.
—THOMAS H. GREEN, SJ[4]

I often do too much talking when I pray. I try to be quiet, but I have too many things to say. Sometimes I barely allow God to get a word in. That's a big mistake, because I know that prayer is a conversation with God. And because he is God, he gets to start it.

We may think we have never heard God speaking to us. But he has been talking to us from the moment he spoke the word that created us from nothing in our mother's womb. From our birth to the present, he has been putting thoughts in our minds and desires in our hearts. So whether we realize it or not, all of our prayer is really a response to God's initiatives.

Prayer, then, is an opening to God, who wants to speak with us. We want to encounter him so that he can engage us in conversation. If that is to happen, when we pray we must first make ourselves aware of God's presence. Coming into God's presence is like looking up from reading the newspaper and noticing that your best friend has entered the room. He has been sitting by the fireplace, desiring a visit. You say his name and acknowledge his presence. Then you begin to converse with him.

I think the best way to begin prayer is by making the sign of the cross. When we pray "in the name of the Father, and of the Son, and of the Holy Spirit," we are addressing God as he has revealed himself to us. Invoking God's name puts us in touch with his divine nature and draws us into his presence. In effect, we are saying, "Lord, I know that you are here. May I have a word with you?" Then our one-on-one conversation with God can begin.

Even when no one else is around, we never pray alone. When we open ourselves to God, we are entering into the prayer of the body of Christ and therefore praying as one body, with the Lord himself and with sisters and brothers in Christ. The reality is that at any moment of the day or night, we can join with millions of Christians who are uniting their hearts and minds to Jesus. We may do that by praying the Liturgy of the Hours, which is Christ's own prayer that sanctifies the various times of the day and evening with psalms, Scripture readings, and prayers. We may pray the Mass readings for that day. Or we may simply make the intention of linking our prayer to the prayer of the church. To do that we may say an invitatory verse like, "O God, come to my assistance. O Lord, make haste to help me." And so we find ourselves praying with the Lord himself and many sisters and brothers.

Prayer is a school that teaches us about God and shows us what he is like. We may think we are only having a one-way dialogue with God when we pray such foundational prayers as the Apostles' Creed, the Lord's Prayer, and the Hail Mary. However, God can speak to us even in these familiar prayers if we listen to their words and seek to understand the truths they express about God.

With the Apostles' Creed, we affirm our faith in the person and work of the holy Trinity. This ancient prayer sums up Christian doctrines about the Father, who created us; Jesus, who saved us and will judge us; and the Holy Spirit, who animates the church with divine life. When we pray the Lord's Prayer, we are asking the Father to establish his kingdom more fully among us and to liberate his creation from the kingdom of his enemy. This prayer renews our decision to collaborate with Christ to bring people into God's kingdom and expresses our reliance on God for provision, forgiveness, and protection as we join the Lord in his great rescue operation. Praying the Hail Mary celebrates our faith in the incarnation, God becoming man in Christ, the central Christian mystery.

We also discover more about God when we pray with Scripture.[5] No surprise there, since the Bible is his living word, spoken to us to draw us into conversation with him. For example, praying the psalms has taught me to honor God for his faithfulness and to reverence him for his justice. With these dispositions of the heart, I am much more receptive to hearing God speak to me. Consider this description of the Lord in Psalm 103, which I turn to often to rekindle my faith and help remind me what God is really like:

> The LORD works vindication
>   and justice for all who are oppressed. . . .
> The LORD is merciful and gracious,
>   slow to anger, and abounding in steadfast love. . . .
> He does not deal with us according to our sins,
>   nor repay us according to our iniquities.
> For as the heavens are high above the earth,
>   so great is his steadfast love toward those who fear him;
> as far as the east is from the west,
>   so far he removes our transgressions from us.
> (Psalm 103:6, 8, 10-12)

Of course, the way we can learn about God in prayer is to actually pray—and that won't happen unless we make sure we carve out time to spend with the Lord. Archbishop Fulton J. Sheen, now a candidate for sainthood, spent one hour every day for sixty years praying in the Lord's presence. He urged everyone to imitate his practice. The archbishop made his holy hour before the Blessed Sacrament. That may not always be possible for us, but we can take extended time in the Lord's presence right in our own homes. In Sheen's autobiography, he told how the practice of making a regular holy hour teaches us about God and draws us nearer to him:

> The purpose of the Holy Hour is to encourage deep personal encounter with Christ. The holy and glorious God is constantly inviting us to come to Him, to converse with Him, to ask for such things as we need and to experience what a blessing there is in fellowship with Him. Sitting before the Presence is like a body exposing itself before the sun to absorb its rays. Silence in the Hour is a tête-à-tête with the Lord.
>
> The Hour also became a teacher for me. Although before we love anyone, we must have knowledge of that person, nevertheless, after we know, it is love that increases knowledge. Theological insights are gained not only from between the two covers of a treatise, but from two knees kneeling in God's presence.[6]

Following Archbishop Sheen's lead, I am trying to spend more time in silence when I pray, giving God a chance to have his say. I hope to get to know him better and so learn to love him more.

—BERT

For Reflection:

What have you learned about God recently from your experience of prayer?

CHAPTER TWENTY-SEVEN

SPIRITUAL READING

A DIALOGUE WITH GOD

Let your minds be filled with everything that is true, everything that is honorable, everything that is upright and pure, everything that we love and admire—with whatever is good and praiseworthy.
—PHILIPPIANS 4:8 (NJB)

The diligent reading of Sacred Scripture accompanied by prayer brings about that intimate dialogue in which the person reading hears God who is speaking, and in praying, responds to him with trusting openness of heart.
—POPE BENEDICT XVI[7]

Today Catholics and other Christians are eagerly recovering the ancient custom of *lectio divina*.[8] This Latin term literally means "divine reading," but it is more commonly translated as "spiritual reading." It refers to the practice of reading and reflecting on Scripture or other spiritual books in a manner that leads to prayerful communication with God. As we read and reflect on God's word, we hear him speaking to us in our thoughts. Then we respond to him in prayer, thus participating in what Pope Benedict XVI has described as an "intimate dialogue" with God. Who could ever want a more interesting and valuable conversation?

Many saints fostered a close relationship with God through the habit of spiritual reading. For example, St. Athanasius

(c. 293–373) meditated on a verse from 1 Corinthians and shared his reflections in his *Life of Anthony:*

> St. Paul became our example for strenuously pursuing holiness when he said, "I die daily" (see 1 Corinthians 15:31). Now, if we were to think each day that we had to die that day, we would never sin at all. If in the morning we imagined that we would never last till evening, and if at evening we thought that we would never see morning, we would never sin.
>
> If we were to keep the imminence of our death in mind, we would never be overcome by sin: lust that is fleeting would not reign over us; we would never harbor anger against another human being; we would not love possessions that pass away; and we would forgive every person who offended us.[9]

Reflecting on Scripture in this way acts like a mirror in which we can view the condition of our Christian lives (see James 1:23-24). Recently I meditated on the way that Joseph of Arimathea buried Jesus and saw some things I should do to strengthen my discipleship (see Matthew 27:57-61). Joseph identified himself with Christ, who had just been executed as a criminal, and asked Pilate for his body, unconcerned about the consequences for himself. I also noticed how Joseph treated the body of Jesus with great reverence and respect and laid it in his own family tomb. As I looked at Joseph, I sensed the Lord calling me to follow him more courageously, worship him more reverently, and serve him more generously. I have a good distance to go to measure up to Joseph's high standards, but I am working on it.

Reading sound spiritual books can also draw us into a closer communication with God. Consider the experience of St. Ignatius of Loyola (1491–1556). As a young man, Ignatius dreamed of a future as a warrior in the service of a king. But an injury sustained during a battle in 1521, when a cannonball shattered his right leg, occasioned a dramatic turnabout in his life.

During his long recovery Ignatius wanted to read romances about knights and their exploits, which he had been addicted to in his youth. However, the only books available to him were two medieval "bestsellers": Ludolph of Saxony's *Life of Christ* and Jacob of Voragine's *The Golden Legend,* which told of the heroism of the saints. Ignatius came to love these books. He especially admired St. Francis of Assisi and St. Dominic, whom he viewed as valiant knights in Christ's service. As he reflected on these saints, he recognized himself in their down-to-earth humanness. He decided that nothing prevented him from imitating their holiness. So spiritual reading launched Ignatius on the road to his conversion and discipleship.

The practice of spiritual reading involves us in a series of movements of mind and heart: reading, meditating, and praying. These movements bring us into conversation with God and prompt us to action—to doing what God tells us to do. We *read* a Scripture text, intent on understanding it. We read with listening ears to hear what God is saying. Then we *meditate* on the text, letting the Holy Spirit show us its message for our lives. Reading and meditating on a text draw us to *pray.* The words we speak in prayer respond to God, who has initiated the conversation in our reading and meditating.

For example, consider how spiritual reading led St. John Gabriel Perboyre (1802–1840) to prayer and action. As a seminarian for the Lazarists, John Gabriel frequently meditated on

Galatians 2:20: "It is no longer I who live, but it is Christ who lives in me." And in response, he regularly prayed this prayer to be like Christ:

O my Divine Savior,
     transform me into yourself.
May my hands be the hands of Jesus.
May my tongue be the tongue of Jesus.
Grant that every faculty of my body
     may serve only to glorify you. . . .
Grant that I may live
     but in you
     and by you
     and for you
     that I may truly say with Saint Paul:
"I live now, not I, but Christ lives in me."[10]

From his youth, John Gabriel wanted to become a missionary to China. And in what seems to have put his prayer into action, in 1835 the Lazarists sent him to their Chinese mission at Honan. Like Christ, two years later, he was martyred between two criminals.[11]

Our spiritual reading may not lead us to martyrdom, but it will surely open us to an intimate dialogue with God and whatever he calls us to do.

—BERT

For Reflection:

What have you learned about God recently in your spiritual reading? Have you shared it with someone?

CHAPTER TWENTY-EIGHT

LEADINGS OF THE SPIRIT

WISDOM, GUIDANCE, AND GRACE

When the Spirit of truth comes, he will guide you into all the truth.
—JOHN 16:13

If we live by the Spirit, let us also be guided by the Spirit.
—GALATIANS 5:25

My wife, Mary Lou, and I have raised seven children. We made many mistakes along the way, but fortunately nothing that we did wrong seems to have permanently damaged any of our sons or daughters.

We also did some things right. Some good parenting practices came naturally. For example, we taught the kids the difference between right and wrong and showed them the importance of living out the two great commandments of loving God and others.

But for many decisions and family policies, we followed wisdom that we did not derive from our own resources. For example, when one of my sons reached adolescence and began to test his limits, I held him to very high standards in every area—eating habits, manners, dress, neatness, schoolwork, morality—you name it. "You are all over him for everything," a friend told me. "If you don't back off, you are going to push him into real rebellion."

You might say that this advice was just good common sense. But in this case, I believe it was wisdom from the highest possible source—the Holy Spirit. For wisdom, which is practical advice for good living, is one of the main gifts the Spirit offers us.

From very early in our marriage, I have prayed daily to the Holy Spirit for help in caring for my family, and I can tell you that it works! Following a traditional formula, I pray

Come, Holy Spirit, fill the hearts of your faithful,
and enkindle in them the fire of your love.
Send forth your Spirit, and they shall be created;
and you shall renew the face of the earth.

O God, who by the light of the Holy Spirit instructs the hearts of the faithful, grant that by the same Spirit we may be truly wise and ever rejoice in his consolation, through Christ our Lord. Amen

I believe that the Holy Spirit prompted my friend to warn me to take the pressure off my son. As I reflected on his advice, I also experienced the Spirit teaching me to hold my son to the highest standard in morality but to allow him plenty of slack in less important areas. So I stopped nagging him about his room and his dress. And this was the consolation I could rejoice in: my relationship with my son improved significantly.

God sends us the Holy Spirit to give us wisdom and guidance for our lives. If we listen attentively, we will hear him speaking to us—not audibly, as sometimes happened with great saints like Francis of Assisi (1181–1226), but we will hear him in our thoughts or through the wisdom of a trusted friend. And we will also hear him in our desires.

Yes, I said *desires*. Sometimes we hold to the myth that says that in order to say yes to God's desires for our lives, we have to say no to our own desires. But the fact is that often our desires come from God. They are one way that the Spirit guides us.

Consider the life of St. Katharine Drexel (1858–1955). From her youth, Katharine wanted to please God. To find the Lord's direction for her life, she prayed daily the *Veni Sancte Spiritus,* the ancient, life-transforming prayer from the Pentecost liturgy. Her heart's desire was to spend her life in contemplative prayer.

That was an early leading of the Spirit, but a most unusual circumstance took her in a very different direction. In 1885 Katharine's father, a wealthy banker, died and left her and her two sisters the annual income from 14 million dollars. Blessed with this huge fortune, she experienced another desire arising in her heart, also a leading of the Spirit, that seemed to conflict with her desire for a life of contemplation. She wanted to give the money to ministries that cared for Native Americans and African-Americans. But her spiritual directors strongly advised her that she needed to serve these marginalized people herself. So she did.

She founded the Sisters of the Blessed Sacrament. For four decades, from 1891 to 1935, she and her associates established 145 missions and 12 schools for Native Americans and 50 schools for African-Americans. Throughout her life she contributed about 20 million dollars for these causes.

After forty years of serving God on his terms, Katharine was granted her youthful wish for a contemplative life of prayer. In 1935 a serious heart attack slowed her down, and two years later she retired. Then she enjoyed eighteen years of quiet contemplation before her death in 1955 at age ninety-seven.[12]

Wisdom and guidance are wonderful leadings of the Spirit. However, alone they are not enough for us, because we need God's help to implement his advice or direction. But we don't have to worry. God loves us so much that he gives us the Holy Spirit to carry us along the path marked out for us. As Paul assured the Romans, we have all the grace we need because "God's love has been poured into our hearts through the Holy Spirit that has been given to us" (Romans 5:5).

—BERT

For Reflection:

In what ways have you experienced receiving wisdom or guidance from the Holy Spirit?

CHAPTER TWENTY-NINE

OBEDIENCE

INTIMACY WITH GOD

This is his commandment, that we should believe in the name of his Son
Jesus Christ and love one another, just as he has commanded us. All who
obey his commandments abide in him, and he abides in them.

—1 JOHN 3:23-24

Contemporary people do not hold obedience in very high regard.
I doubt I would get much argument if I asserted that it is the least
popular of all the virtues. We place a very high premium on our
autonomy because we believe that making our own choices guar-
antees our freedom. In my late teens, when I was testing my wings,
my independent spirit frustrated my poor mother. "Do what you
want," she would say. "You will anyway!" And to be candid, I
still struggle with obedience. For example, I don't like it when
my wife seems to be telling me what to do.

It's a mistake to regard obedience as the enemy of freedom.
Just the opposite is the case. In all human enterprises, obedience
enables us to be free. To excel at softball, for example, a player
must discipline herself to obey the rules of the game, the coach's
directions, the game plan, the team's exercise and training program, and the umpire's decisions. If she obeys these things, she is
free to do well at the sport. If not, she will not only play poorly,
but as a renegade she will win the disfavor of coach and team-
mates and find herself on the bench or the street. So autonomy,
not obedience, is really the enemy of freedom.

For the Christian, obedience has an even more significant benefit. Scripture teaches that obeying the commandments brings us into intimacy with God. "Anyone who loves me will keep my word, and my Father will love him, and we shall come to him and make a home in him" (John 14:23, NJB). Nothing could be more intimate than the Father and the Son coming to dwell personally in an obedient heart. So obedience and spiritual intimacy are two sides of the same coin.

"Now wait a minute!" you might say. "I obey all the commandments, but I don't feel very close to God. What am I missing?" I used to feel the same way. And I can assure you that you are not missing anything. For several years, I wondered why my faithfulness to the commandments did not reward me with the intimacy with God that Scripture promised. A prominent message of contemporary Christian culture heightened my sense of failure. "Finding intimacy with God" had become a buzzword among Christian writers at the turn of the millennium. But no matter how hard I tried, I didn't find it.

Then one day it dawned on me. I was projecting a romantic idea of intimacy from human relationships onto my relationship with God. I was expecting to experience a set of heartfelt feelings of closeness to the Lord. Big mistake. That would be nice, and it may happen. But that's not what Jesus intended when he said that obedience to the commandments leads to intimacy with God.

God does come to be with a person who loves him and obeys his commandment to love others. But that intimacy reflects the objective relationship between master and disciple, not the subjective intimacy of lovers. Here's what Jesus had to say on the subject: "If any want to become my followers, let them deny themselves and take up their cross daily and follow me" (Luke 9:23). Getting close to Jesus means agreeing to share in his suffering.

Thus, loving and obeying the Lord require a cost, and so may involve feelings of fear and loss—feelings that we may experience as much as the joy and comradeship we expect.

As paradoxical as it may seem, the intimacy with God that comes from obedience may carry with it a sense of aloneness or abandonment. We see this most in the man Jesus Christ, who felt during his crucifixion that God had forsaken him, although God was with him through it all. And we observe it in the lives of many saints who, though obedient lovers of God and humanity, felt distant from or even abandoned by him.

Consider the experience of St. Alphonsus Ligouri (1696–1787). Opposition dogged St. Alphonsus for the last sixty years of his life. Anticlericals battled the Redemptorists, the order he had founded. Jansenist heretics denounced him and the book he wrote to correct them. Rheumatism bent his head into his neck, a deformity he endured for his last twenty years. A controversy between the pope and the king of Naples over the Redemptorist rule resulted in his exclusion from the very order he had founded. And for eighteen months just before he died, Alphonsus suffered a dark period of doubts, fears, and scruples.

The saint was intimate with God as a collaborator in defending the faith, but he did not depend on experiencing God's presence. Alphonsus offered his obedience as the cost of his discipleship and did not expect consolations. He believed that God drew close to him not to comfort him but to smooth his rough edges. As he once said, "Contradictions, sickness, scruples, spiritual aridity and all the inner and outward torments are the chisel with which God carves his saints for paradise."[13]

So if we desire intimacy with God, we should love him and obey his commandments, and we will enjoy closeness to him, whether we feel it or not. That's the benefit of obedience. Then when God pulls out the chisel that he always carries, we should just sit still and let him chip away at our faults. That's the cost.

—BERT

For Reflection:

In what ways has obedience to God drawn you closer to him?

CHAPTER THIRTY

WHAT OUR EXPERIENCE TEACHES US ABOUT GOD

SETTING OUR SPIRITUAL ANTENNA

*In the winter, seeing a tree stripped of its leaves, and considering that
within a little time the leaves would be renewed
and after that the flowers and fruit appear,
Brother Lawrence received a high view of the Providence and Power
of God, which has never been erased from his soul.*[14]
—THE PRACTICE OF THE PRESENCE OF GOD

As we come to the end of our reflections, we must now stop and
ask, "What can our everyday experience teach us about God?"
We have looked around us and have seen traces of his greatness
in the beauty of the earth, the glory of the heavens, the intrica-
cies of our bodies, and the majesty of art and architecture. We
have sensed his love in our deepest longings and in our families
and friends. We have noted our likeness to him in the creativity
of our work and in our hunger for justice.

We have contemplated the nearness of eternity in our present moments. We have seen God's goodness overflow in acts of
kindness and chances for fresh starts. We have celebrated his
bringing good from evil in the relief of suffering and the grant-
ing of forgiveness.

We have remembered that God is speaking to us; that he has
revealed himself to us in Scripture; that by looking at Jesus, we can

see what the Father is like; that theology can nourish our mind and heart; and that the Eucharist nourishes our spirits. And we have realized that God still intervenes in our lives with miracles.

Finally, we have noticed all the ordinary ways that we communicate with God and become close to him—by listening, by conversing with him in prayer, by reading Scripture as his word to us, by considering what he wants of us, and by doing what he tells us.

By taking you through all of these considerations in this book, Bert and I wanted to raise your awareness of the many different ways that God is in touch with you. We hope that you will continue to reflect on your experiences in meeting God in ordinary daily ways.

We all should aspire to be like Brother Lawrence (c. 1605–1691), the Carmelite brother and mystic who, at age eighteen, encountered God by meditating on a barren tree in winter. As he reflected on the rebirth of the tree in spring, he was so deeply touched by God's providence and power that he was forever changed. This ordinary encounter opened him to experience God's presence daily for the rest of his life.

I invite you to set your spiritual antenna to pick up all the signals that communicate God's presence to you. The Lord taught us in Scripture how to stay alert to his nearness and his concern for us. "Set your hearts on his kingdom first, and on God's saving justice, and all these other things will be given you as well" (Matthew 6:33, NJB). Deciding or renewing your decision to put God first in your life will make you receptive to him in everyday circumstances. That's how you can activate your spiritual antenna to receive the flow of God's communications to you.

I also suggest that you take some time, perhaps in the evening just before bedtime, to reflect on your day and ask questions like these: "In what ways did I sense God's presence today? Was I in tune with his voice?" Encountering God in our experiences brings us great benefits. It makes us more receptive to his graces as well as more grateful for them. And attentiveness to his presence calls us to a more meaningful observance of our faith and a more faithful exercise of our discipleship.

The first biographer of Brother Lawrence summed up the saint's work in a sentence that serves as a fitting conclusion to our considerations:

> God is everywhere, in all places, and there is no spot where we cannot draw near to Him, and hear Him speaking in our heart; with a little *love*, just a very little, we shall not find it hard.[15]

—Fr. Benedict

For Reflection:

When were you most aware of God's presence today?

QUESTIONS FOR GROUP DISCUSSION

1. Why can listening to life help you grow in prayer?

2. In what sense can you say that you never pray alone?

3. In what ways has spiritual reading advanced you in Christian living?

4. How have you experienced the Holy Spirit leading or helping you?

5. When has your obedience to God led to more intimacy with him?

6. What one decision can you make to assure that you will experience God in your daily life?

NOTES

Part One / All around Us (pp. 11–36)

1. "Francis of Assisi: Writer" in Marion A. Habig, ed., *St. Francis of Assisi: Writings and Early Biographies, English Omnibus of the Sources for the Life of St. Francis* (Chicago: Franciscan Herald Press, 1983), 1922.

2. George Martin, "Creation," *God's Word Today*, June 1998, 42.

3. www.nasa.gov/worldbook/star_worldbook.html.

4. www.nasa.gov/worldbook/star_worldbook.html.

5. Ron Cowen, "Evidence for a Distant Galaxy Cluster," *Science News*, February 12, 1994, findarticles.com.

6. Martin, 46; George F. Will, "The Gospel from Science," *Newsweek*, November 9, 1998, 88.

7. Will, 88.

8. Alexander Tsiaras and Barry Werth, *From Conception to Birth: A Life Unfolds*, quoted in J. Madeleine Nash, "Inside the Womb," *Time*, November 11, 2002, www.time.com.

9. "Inside the Womb."

10. See Jean Vanier, "As My Heart Opens Up," in *Eruption to Hope* (Toronto: Griffin House, 1971), 105.

11. Pope John Paul II, General Audience, February 20, 1980, www.vatican.va/holy_father/john_paul_ii/audiences /catechesis_genesis/documents/hf_jp-ii_aud_19800220_en.html.

12. Bert Ghezzi, *Voices of the Saints* (New York: Doubleday, 2000), 121, 592.

13. Briege McKenna, OSC, and Henry Libersat, *Miracles Do Happen* (Cincinnati, OH: Servant Books, 1996), 2–5 passim.

14. Cross International draft advertorial for the *Florida Catholic* (undated), left page.

15. J. K. Rowling, *Harry Potter and the Deathly Hallows* (New York: Scholastic, Inc., 2007).

16. Mother Teresa, *Mother Teresa: Come Be My Light,* ed. Brian Kolodiejchuk (New York: Doubleday, 2007).

17. Thomas Dubay, *The Evidential Power of Beauty* (San Francisco: Ignatius Press, 1999), 56.

Part Two / A Look in the Mirror (pp. 37–62)

1. Augustine, *Confessions*, 10.27.

2. C. S. Lewis, *The Four Loves* (London: Fontana Books, 1973), 13.

3. *Spiritual Friendship,* cited in and trans. Aelred Squire, *Aelred of Rievaulx: A Study* (London: SPCK, 1973), 49–50.

4. This "Instruction to the Marrying Couple at the Beginning of the Wedding Ceremony" was a standard part of the liturgy of matrimony when we were married in 1964. See it cited in *Liguorian*, June 1987, 16.

5. Pope John Paul II, *Letter to Artists,* 1, www.vatican .va/holy_father/john_paul_ii/letters/documents/ hf_jp-ii_let_23041999_artists_en.html.

6. Quoted at www.brainyquote.com/quotes/authors/p/pablo _picasso.html.

7. Paul Johnson, *Creators* (New York: HarperCollins Publishers, 2006), 250.

8. Quoted at oaks.nvg.org/picasso.html.

9. Studs Terkel, *Working* (New York: Pantheon Books, 1974), xlvi.

10. Terkel, xlix.

11. Johnson, 3.

12. N. T. Wright, *Simply Christian* (San Francisco: HarperSanFrancisco, 2006), 4.

Part Three / Everyday Experiences (pp. 63–89)

1. Jean-Pierre de Caussade, *The Abandonment to Divine Providence* (New York: Doubleday, 1966), cited at landru.i-link-2.net/shnyves/Quotes_from_de_Caussade.html.

2. *Letters of St. Jerome,* 77.6.

3. Quoted in Bert Ghezzi, *Voices of the Saints* (New York: Doubleday, 2000), 112.

4. On September 14, 2002, the Congregation for the Causes of Saints opened the cause for the canonization of Archbishop Fulton J. Sheen. As the first step in the process, the congregation conferred on him the title "Servant of God."

5. Paul Scott, "The Friendship," *The Guideposts Treasury of Love* (New York: Bantam, 1982), 261.

6. Anne Herbert, *Random Kindness and Senseless Acts of Beauty* (Volcano, CA: Volcano Press, 1993).

7. See, for example, www.helpothers.org/ and www.actsofkindness.org/.

8. This chapter is based on an interview with Fr. Ed Thompson, June 8, 2007, and on "A Priest Alcoholic Tells His Story," in Henry Libersat, *Miracles Today* (Ann Arbor, Michigan: Servant Publications, 1999), 169–181.

9. Interview.

10. Interview.

11. Libersat, 170.

12. Libersat, 170.

13. Interview.

14. Interview.

15. Interview.

16. Libersat, 181.

17. "Life of Reilly: Coaching the Grief Stricken," *Sports Illustrated*, April 30, 2007, back page.

18. Quoted in Jarrett Bell, "Tragedy forces Dungy to 'live in the present,'" *USA Today*, www.usatoday.com/sports/football/nfl/colts/2006-08-31-dungy-cover_x.htm.

19. Quoted in Bell, *USA Today*.

20. Quoted in "Life of Reilly."

21. "Life of Reilly."

22. Quoted in "Life of Reilly."

23. "Tony Dungy Super Bowl Breakfast 2006, Part 2," www.youtube.com/watch?v=K3PUPCR7NFA&mode=related&search=.

24. "Tony Dungy Super Bowl Breakfast."

25. Nick Cavnar, "Jim Elliot: Apostle to the Aucas," *New Covenant*, May 1980, 9–12.

26. Quoted in Elisabeth Elliot, *The Shadow of the Almighty: The Life and Testimony of Jim Elliott* (San Francisco: HarperSanFrancisco, 1989), 177.

27. Quoted in Cavnar, 12.

28. Interview with Kathryn Deering, Elisabeth Elliot's book editor. Once when Kathryn was visiting at her home, Elisabeth showed her the spear and explained its significance.

29. Pope Benedict XVI, *Spe Salve*, 5, www.vatican.va/holy_father/benedict_xvi/encyclicals/documents/hf_ben-xvi_enc_20071130_spe-salvi_en.html.

30. Cited in Pope Benedict XVI, *Spe Salve*, 3.

Part Four / Real Presence (pp. 91–117)

1. Pope Benedict XVI, *Jesus of Nazareth* (New York: Doubleday, 2007), 44.

2. Francis S. Collins, "Why This Scientist Believes in God," www.cnn.com/2007/US/04/03/collins.commentary.

3. *Butler's Lives of the Saints: New Full Edition* (Collegeville, MN: The Liturgical Press, 1995), 117.

4. *The Confessions of St. Augustine,* trans. John K. Ryan (New York: Doubleday Image Books, 1960), 8.12.29.

5. Bert Ghezzi, *The Heart of a Saint* (Ijamsville, MD: The Word Among Us Press, 2007), 48.

6. Anthony Cassano, "The First Day of My Life of Faith," in Louise Perrotta, *His Word Is Among Us* (Ijamsville, MD: The Word Among Us Press, 2004), 55–57. A pseudonym has been used at the author's request.

7. Cassano, 56.

8. Cassano, 57.

9. N. T. Wright, *Simply Christian* (San Francisco: HarperSanFrancisco, 2006), 140.

10. Wright, 138.

11. Frank J. Sheed, *Theology and Sanity* (San Francisco: Ignatius Press, 1978), 7.

12. Sheed, *Theology and Sanity,* 27.

13. F[rank] J. Sheed, *Theology for Beginners* (Ann Arbor, MI: Servant Books, 1981), 4.

14. Sheed, *Theology and Sanity,* 23–25.

15. *The Oxford Dictionary of the Christian Church*, 2nd edition, ed. F. L. Cross and E. A. Livingstone (New York: Oxford University Press, 1990), 31.

16. *Butler's Lives of the Saints: New Full Edition*, 56. See also Bert Ghezzi, *Mystics and Miracles* (Chicago: Loyola Press, 2002), 89.

17. Sheed, *Theology and Sanity,* 7.

18. *Real People, Real Presence,* intro. Cardinal William H. Keeler (Ijamsville, MD: The Word Among Us Press, 2004), 32–35.

19. *Real People,* 33.

20. *Real People,* 33.

21. *Catechism of the Catholic Church,* 1324, quoting *Lumen gentium* 11, www.vatican.va/archive/ /hist_councils /ii_vatican_council/documents/vat-ii_const_19641121_lumen -gentium_en.html.

22. *Catechism,* 1324, quoting *Presbyterorum ordinis 5.*

23. Dorothy Day, "Liturgy and Sociology," *The Catholic Worker,* January 1936, 5, www.catholicworker.org/dorothyday. See also Bert Ghezzi, *The Heart of a Saint* (Ijamsville, MD: The Word Among us Press, 2007), 81–82.

24. Benedict Groeschel, CFR, *The Journey Toward God* (Ann Arbor, MI: Servant Publications, 2000), 180–182.

Part Five / Communication with God (pp. 119–144)

1. Benedict J. Groeschel, CFR, *Listening at Prayer* (New York: Paulist Press, 1983), 8.

2. See Proverbs 21:13.

3. Thomas Merton, *Conjectures of a Guilty Bystander,* www.law .louisville.edu/cardinallawyer/node/61/.

4. Thomas H. Green, SJ, *Opening to God* (New York: Bantam Books, 1987), 25–26.

5. See Chapter 27, "Spiritual Reading," 129–132.

6. Adapted from *Treasure in Clay: The Autobiography of Fulton J. Sheen* (Garden City, NY: Doubleday & Company, 1980), 190–194.

7. Pope Benedict XVI, addressing participants of the International Congress on the 40th Anniversary of *Dei Verbum,* Rome, September 16, 2005, www.vatican.va/holy_father /benedict_xvi/speeches/2005/september/documents/hf_ben ß-xvi_spe_20050916_40-dei-verbum_en.html.

8. For an excellent introduction to the practice of *lectio divina,* see Stephen J. Binz, *Conversing with God in Scripture: A Contemporary Approach to Lectio Divina* (Ijamsville, MD: The Word Among Us Press, 2008).

9. Adapted from Athanasius, *The Life of St. Anthony* in *The Paradise or Garden of the Holy Fathers,* vol. 1 (Seattle: Saint Nectarios Press, 1978), 20.

10. G. de Montgesty, *Two Vincentian Martyrs,* adapt. Florence Gilmore (Maryknoll, NY: Catholic Foreign Mission Society of America, 1925), 127.

11. See St. John Gabriel Perboyre's story in Bert Ghezzi, *Voices of the Saints* (New York: Doubleday, 2000), 372–373.

12. For a fuller account of St. Katharine Drexel's dual vocation to prayer and action, see Bert Ghezzi, *The Heart of a Saint* (Ijamsville, MD: The Word Among Us Press, 2007), 53–64.

13. Bert Ghezzi, *Voices of the Saints* (New York: Doubleday, 2000), 20–21.

14. Adapted from Brother Lawrence, *The Practice of the Presence of God* (New York: Cosimo, 2006), 6.

15. *The Practice of the Presence of God,* 72 (emphasis in original).

ACKNOWLEDGMENTS

Unless otherwise noted, Scriptures are from the New Revised Standard Version Bible: Catholic Edition, copyright ©1989 by the Division of Christian Education of the National Council of the Churches of Christ in the U.S.A. All rights reserved. Used with permission.

Scripture texts marked NJB are taken from the New Jerusalem Bible, copyright © 1985 by Darton, Longman & Todd, Ltd., and Doubleday, a division of Bantam Doubleday Dell Publishing Group, Inc. Reprinted by permission.

Scripture texts marked NIV are taken from the Holy Bible, New International Version®. Copyright © 1973, 1978, 1984 International Bible Society. Used by permission of Zondervan. All rights reserved. The "NIV" and "New International Version" trademarks are registered in the United States Patent and Trademark Office by International Bible Society. Use of either trademark requires the permission of International Bible Society.

Scriptures texts marked NAB are taken from the New American Bible with Revised New Testament and Revised Psalms, copyright © 1991, 1986, 1970 Confraternity of Christian Doctrine, Washington, D.C. and are used by permission of the copyright owner. All Rights Reserved. No part of the New American Bible may be reproduced in any form without permission in writing from the copyright owner.

Quotations from the English translation of the *Catechism of the Catholic Church* for use in the United States of America, copyright © 1994, United States Catholic Conference, Inc.—Libreria Editrice Vaticana. Used with permission.